Saving the
NORTH COAST
REDWOODS

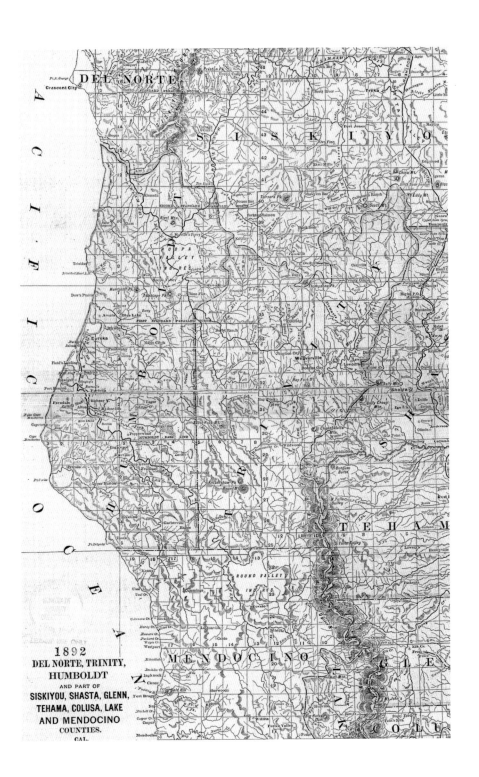

1892
DEL NORTE, TRINITY,
HUMBOLDT
AND PART OF
SISKIYOU, SHASTA, GLENN,
TEHAMA, COLUSA, LAKE
AND MENDOCINO
COUNTIES.
CAL.

Saving the
NORTH COAST
REDWOODS

Susan J.P. O'Hara

THE
History
PRESS

Published by The History Press
Charleston, SC
www.historypress.com

Cover images: A Model T parked in the redwood forest along Bull Creek exemplifies experiences of the SRL founders in 1917. *HRIA*; members of the Humboldt Save the Redwoods pose in front of a vehicle. *HHS*; logging partners Ted Morris (*top*) and Lloyd Sublett (*bottom right*) of Morris-Sublett pose with large log felled near present-day Cutten, near Eureka. *Ted Morris*.

Frontispiece: This 1892 map of northwestern California illustrates the remote location of redwoods in Northern and Southern Humboldt and in Del Norte Counties. *CPHLSC*.

First published 2024

Manufactured in the United States

ISBN 9781467157131

Library of Congress Control Number: 2023950641

Notice: The information in this book is true and complete to the best of our knowledge. It is offered without guarantee on the part of the author or The History Press. The author and The History Press disclaim all liability in connection with the use of this book.

This book is dedicated to past, present and future California state and national park rangers and staff who work to protect, preserve and rebuild the redwood forest. It is also dedicated to my husband, who has been both a logger and a state park employee and shares my love of the redwoods.

CONTENTS

The Humboldt Redwoods Interpretive Association was created in 1979 to provide interpretation and information about Humboldt Redwoods State Park. The association opened a visitor center staffed by volunteers the following year. Since that time, the association has helped millions of travelers to better understand the uniqueness of Humboldt Redwoods State Park. It now operates four visitor centers: at Humboldt Redwoods, Richardson Grove, Sinkyone Wilderness and Grizzly Creek State Park. The author is donating her royalties to HRIA to support it in its ongoing efforts to inform about the redwoods. *Courtesy the author.*

ACKNOWLEDGEMENTS

The author would like to thank the California State Department of Parks and Recreations archives and current and past state park rangers who have helped with this book. These include Thomas Valterria, Sam Rich, Rick Sermon, Ron Jones and Jim Baird, who have shared tales of being a ranger and pictures of their work. Additionally, thanks to the Cal Poly Humboldt Library Special Collections (CPHLSC) for its generous use of images, as well as to Cal Poly Humboldt professor Steven Sillett, Humboldt Redwoods Interpretive Association (HRIA), the California State Park Archives (CSPA), the Humboldt Historical Society (HCHS) and the Fortuna Depot Museum (FDM). Additional sources include oral histories, newspaper archives and other primary and secondary sources. Author royalties are being donated to the Humboldt Redwoods Interpretive Association to benefit its mission to interpret the redwoods. Thank you to the reader for your interest in the redwoods.

INTRODUCTION

The majority of the California State Redwood Parks are located in Humboldt and Del Norte Counties, in the northwest portion of the state. This is no accident. The redwood groves in the region were isolated from lumber mills until they were preserved by the actions of the Save the Redwoods League (SRL), following a tour of the area in 1917. Indeed, the SRL was formed due to the destruction the founders of the league—Madison Grant, John Merriam and Henry Osborn—observed on this trip to the redwoods of northwestern California. Fortuitously, the trees along the South Fork of the Eel were inaccessible for the first sixty years of Euro-American settlement, since trees closer to the mills were more easily harvested. The same holds for the trees in Northern Humboldt and the forests in Del Norte County. Moreover, in Southern Humboldt, the Eel was too challenging to float logs on, as had been done in other parts of the country. Yet by the late 1910s, the protection offered by the redwoods' distance from mills was disappearing; in 1914, the Northwestern Pacific Railroad was completed, and the Redwood Highway was under construction. In Del Norte County, the lumber industry also depended on trains, as well as logging those trees closest to Crescent City. Logging with trucks changed the dynamics following World War II; by then, the SRL was already active in purchasing groves to preserve for all.

The Save the Redwoods League began with the simple yet worthy mission and goal of protecting the redwoods of Northern California

Pictured is redwood logging, split products and the Northwestern Pacific Railroad, which hauled logs and products to markets in the late 1910s. *Library of Congress.*

from the possibility of extinction. The threat to the trees was concrete; the majestic trees were being logged not only for lumber but also for grapestakes, shingle bolts and railroad ties, all products that could be taken to the railroad to be shipped from the remote locations along the South Fork of the Eel. The Northwestern Pacific Railroad had started to be extended south toward the region in 1907. Earlier, The Pacific Lumber Company (TPLCo) had pushed the line south to Shively. From there, spurs, some with temporary trestles, were built, allowing access to groves of trees on both sides of the river. The harvested trees were hauled to mills located at Scotia and around Humboldt Bay to be made into timber. By 1910, the tracks had reached Dyerville, the junction of the South Fork and Main Fork of the Eel. A railroad depot was created at South Fork, just to the east of what is now Founder's Grove. It was to this location that ties, shingle bolts, grapestakes and other split products were taken to be shipped to markets.

In 1922, J.D. Grant observed, "[T]he redwoods belong to the nation, yet Humboldt County may well be proud of the distinction she receives because these matchless forests happen to be located here."[1] The founders of the SRL were shocked by inroads loggers were making in the forest, concerned that the redwoods were being rapidly depleted. Thus, they

worked to preserve the trees they found endangered for future generations to enjoy. The trees along the South Fork and main stem of the Eel River, as well as the Van Duzen, were all being logged at an increasing rate—road construction damaging the fragile root systems of the giants. Madison Grant, in his article in the *New York Zoological Bulletin* in 1919, describes the redwood as being "a beautiful, cheerful and very brave tree."[2] Thanks to his efforts and others interested in redwood preservation and the State of California, many of these groves of beautiful, cheerful and brave trees have been preserved. Several of the first groves preserved have reached their centennial, continuing to be preserved for future generations. The history of the Redwood State Parks in northwestern California begins then with the redwood trees themselves and their unique characteristics that made redwood lumber and split products in high demand during the end of the nineteenth century and the beginning of the twentieth, thus attracting the attention of those who realized the need to preserve them.

Although during the initial Euro-American settlement of Humboldt Bay in 1850, residents found the trees too large to manage, by the mid-1850s, mill owners had discovered that the tall trees could be harvested and sawn with the advancing technology of the era. Redwood quickly found a market around the world. To access this market, most of the mills

Redwoods appear ethereal in this 1910 picture, exemplifying Thornton's observation: "The sequoia stands in the hush of an absolute calm." *Library of Congress.*

from 1855 to 1890 were built around Humboldt Bay, far from the banks of the South Fork or Prairie Creek. Although it's a soft wood, tannin in the wood made it impervious to many insects. A friable wood, it easily split into a variety of products, such as railroad ties, grapestakes and shingles. The split products were so popular, in fact, that many mills operated a shingle mill in addition to their regular lumber sawmill. Other uses of redwood included tanks, coffins, furniture, cigar boxes and musical instruments. The wood was very tight-grained, with as much as fifty rings to an inch, and straight-grained for woodworking. For the lumbermen, redwood represented money, with the redwood lumber earning the moniker "red gold." In 1897, the Redwood Lumber Manufactures Association published a "Souvenir of the Redwood Lumber Industry" touting the trees' attributes: "[I]t is a beautiful lumber, wide and clear. It has a quality as distinct as the territory in which it grows."[3] The text also noted "the endurance of redwood and its resistance to decay are qualities that make it superior to other woods for various purposes."[4] Lumber owners also reminded buyers of the wood's rich colors, observing that "there is considerable variety in shades from a light cherry to a dark mahogany….When once finished there is no material which changes so little and retains its gloss and beauty than the redwood." Finally, in addition to being straight-grained, the wood "had little shrinkage in drying, and once seasoned it is not at all affected by the changes of climate. On this account it is in demand for patterns, and models for castings, for panels and styles for doors…no wood is easily worked or will remain so perfectly and securely in place without shrinkage and swelling as redwood."[5] The wood's popularity, and commensurate

sales, made mill owners rich, garnering them the name "lumber barons." For these men and those who worked in the woods and mills, the trees were thought of in terms of saw logs and board feet. One millworker, Martin Brinzing, who started working in the Caspar Lumber Company in 1904 when he was thirteen to support his family, observed upon seeing the Founder's Tree, in the early 1960s, "[M]y god, there are three saw logs to the first limb."[6] He was not thinking that the tree should be cut, but merely putting it in terms he understood.

Another perspective of the trees is found in Delmar Thornbury's 1926 *California's Redwood Wonderland, Humboldt County*. He feels that the "wonderful redwood forests of Humboldt County…will be recognized by all people, as one of the natural wonders of the world." He continues:

> *A drive through the forest makes man a pygmy. Their proportions are perfect and gradually as you look and see the comparison of size with the objects around you, the sequoia swell and swell, until in the midst of the grandeur, such sublimity of nature, how insignificant one feels himself to be. Immense gray trunks in the gray fog, stand like sentinels of the ages, which have sprung up from unknown depths and are patiently waiting the time when their immense growth shall lift them into another world. They dream, their thoughts are too full of other weightier things to enter fully into little plans. Starting from a base lost in a bed of ferns, we follow with our eyes the great furrows plowed in the red green stained bark to the sturdy limbs with their feathery leaves. The branches start directly, but at the ends sweep downward as though embracing the trunks. Here*

The Founder's Tree, dedicated to the founders of the Save the Redwoods League, towers over the viewer. *HRIA.*

is size, dignity, and stillness. How absolutely and how all pervading, almost supernatural in their profound stillness. These trees do not sway in the wind, they are constructed to stand solid. Their fine turned needles may catch the breeze, but you and I are too far below to distinguish the whisperings. The sequoia stands in the hush of an absolute calm.[7]

The redwoods seem to encourage speaking in superlatives, often described as awe-inspiring, as being a living cathedral, as unique among trees. Another testament to the trees by Wallace Atwood, president of the National Parks Association in 1931, noted the trees' impact:

They form with their branches, huge Gothic arches which reach ever higher and higher toward the heavens. They so interfere with the direct rays of the sun that in the depths of the forest the light is subdued and like that of twilight. On the floor at many places in the midst of these wonderful groves, there are soft carpets of dark-brown needles or of the deep green leaves of the growing oxalis.[8]

Chapter 1

THE REDWOODS

Relics from the Triassic Age, redwood trees have specialized attributes due to having developed 240 million years ago that continue to aid in their survival. Dr. W.L. Jepson of the University of California–Berkeley observed in 1922 that "more than forty five species of redwood have been described from the fossil beds....Some twelve species grew in North America. They grew in France, Switzerland, Austria, Bohemia, Germany, England." Redwoods once covered large portions of what is now North America but now are only found naturally in a small band along the coastal ranges in California near Monterey extending as far north as the Chetco River in Oregon. Despite their size, the trees are similar to a hothouse flower, requiring moderate temperatures, a nutrient-rich soil and frequent moisture. The *Stockton Daily Evening Record* in 1922 noted that Dr. Jepson felt "the scientific interest of the redwood is undoubtedly greater than that of any other cone-bearing class."[9] Research continues to provide new insights into the giants.

Scientifically, the trees are classified as being in the genus *Sequoia*, in the cypress family. Though related to the *Sequoia gigantea* and the dawn redwood, the *Metasequoia*, the *Sempervirens* are the only tree in the genus *Sequoia*. Debate has arisen in the first quarter of the twenty-first century about the origin of the name *Sequoia*. A long-held belief promotes that it comes from Chief Sequoyah, who invented the written Cherokee language. A new theory proposes that botanist Stephen L. Endlicher named the genus *Sequoia* "in the framework of 'the science of his times in the Austrian Empire.'"[10] Gary

Fossilized redwood branchlets were found in Wyoming in 1902. The branchlets appear almost identical to branchlets found among the redwoods today. *Courtesy the author.*

Lowe has concluded that, given Endlicher's knowledge of Latin and its use in creating Botanical Latin,

> *with the name of the genus Sequoia Endlicher's Linnaean botanical nomenclatural practices and his understanding of the ancient Latin of the manuscript texts allowed him to readily use as a prefix "sequo" the early root of the Latin verb "sequor" by dropping the added "r" and then adding the Latin suffix "ia" to yield the new word Sequoia as the name for the genus of conifers that followed within his sequence, Endlicher's Sequence, of five genera in his Suborder Cunninghamieae; trees that he had never seen in a mature state and was unaware of their precise geographic location or habitat.* [11]

It would seem that like Shakespeare's rose, a *Sequoia* of whatever nomenclature remains unique and beautiful.

All agree that the *Semperviren* portion, meaning "ever living" in Latin, is due to the tree's ability to survive diseases and fire that cause other trees to die. The bark and wood are impervious to insect attacks due to tannins in the wood, and the bark is fire resistant. The wood itself, with its reddish

A redwood slab reveals the red interior wood, giving it its eponymous name, as well as the bark's reddish hue. *Author image.*

Cal-Poly Humboldt professor Steve Sillett's photo of the canopy in Humboldt Redwoods State Park captures its unique qualities. *Steven Sillett.*

color, gives the tree its common name and also helps the tree to live for many centuries, as the core wood acts as a storage unit of water for the tree. The Spanish explorers called the giant tree "Palo Colorado," and "redwood" has been the general term for the tall trees since. The fire-resistant bark and tannins combine to make the lifespans of redwoods impressive. Redwoods commonly found in an old-growth forest range in age from seedlings to giants that have lived eight hundred to one thousand years. Some of the fallen trees' rings indicate that a few trees have exceeded two thousand years on the planet. When writing about the coastal redwood and its range, U.C. Berkeley botanist Willis Jepson observed that "the region of this great coniferous forest is a very attractive one, regarded from almost any point of view, and delights the eye and mind of the tourist as well as the botanical traveler."[12]

All parts of the tree work together, aiding in its ability to live for millennia. Starting at the top of the tree, the crown forms the canopy of the forest. In the canopy, branches intertwine, bonding together, allowing for moisture to be shared. The interconnection also provides support. As a result, the tree's trunk near the crown is often split, forming several trunks near the top of the tree. One tree studied by Stephen Sillett of Cal Poly Humboldt and Robert Van Pelt of the University of Washington, Seattle, had 134 reiterated crowns—meaning branches of the tree had turned into trunks as well. One branch or trunk reiterated itself six times. The reiterations and branches create places for needles and small branches to accumulate, providing habitat for salamanders, birds and flying squirrels. One sea bird, the marbled murrelet, flies from the ocean to make its nests in the old-growth trees. Owls, such as the spotted owl, also make homes in the tall trees. As a result, the biomass of an old-growth forest "can exceed 3,000 metric tons per hectare,"[13] according to Van Pelt and Sillett. Thus, an old-growth redwood forest has the greatest terrestrial biomass. Many redwoods grow to a height of 200 to 300 feet. The Hyperion, the tallest measured redwood, is 380 feet tall. Competition for light is one of the driving forces for the height of the tree. Other factors include the nutrient-rich duff of the forest floor and annual rains providing large amounts of moisture for the trees. In Rockefeller Forest, in Humboldt Redwoods State Park, there is seven times more biomass per acre than in a jungle. Rockefeller Forest, according to Guinness World Records, "contains 130 trees that are greater than 351 feet tall…including 11 that stand taller than 361 feet. This equates to a density of one greater than 351 foot tree for every 6.4 acres." The organization also notes that old-growth redwood forests can "store 2,866 tons of carbon per hectare."[14]

Some of the carbon is found in fallen and decaying trees that, along with dropped needles and branches, compose the forest floor. A tree takes many decades to decompose, slowly releasing nutrients stored in the tree back to the surrounding forest. A fallen tree opens up a new space in the canopy, allowing smaller trees opportunities for daylight they may otherwise not have had. It becomes what is referred to as a "mother tree," providing space for ferns, oxalis and other plants to grow. Branches, if the tree is still rooted, grow into new trees, relying on nourishment provided from the fallen giant. If not rooted, the tree's length can be a site for seeds to sprout and grow into the gap left by the fallen tree. The canopy of the forest itself is sloped, with the tallest trees in the middle of a stand of trees and the shortest at the edges, thus dispersing the wind's force through interconnected crowns.

Another key to the redwood's survival are the roots of the tree. Instead of having a deep tap root, redwoods have developed another method to withstand high winds. A network of roots, like the branches near the crown, spread out from the base of the tree up to one hundred feet, interconnecting

This "mother tree"—a fallen log supporting growth of ferns, oxalis and small trees—also highlights the wide spreading roots. *CSPA.*

with the roots from other trees. Thus the trees sway but also help one another to remain standing. The roots range in size from large branch size to small rootlets the thickness of a human hair. Though widespread, the roots delve into the forest floor only about six feet. The roots remain close to the surface to absorb water dripped from the upper branches. The roots' main function is to supply water and nutrients to the tree, thus they are vital to the trees' survival. Damage to the root system can kill a redwood, despite its other invulnerabilities, and thus currently popular named trees, such as the Founder's Tree, are often surrounded by a deck so the roots are not trampled. Similarly, after a large flood, thick deposits of silt can kill a tree,

Redwood cones and seeds, with a nickel for size comparison. At one time, redwood seeds were collected to help large mills' replanting efforts. *Author image.*

and early road construction in the 1910s and '20s both allowed access to see the large stands of trees in Humboldt and Del Norte Counties but also damaged and killed many trees.

Redwoods reveal their ancient heritage by having male and female flowers on different branches, relying on wind and gravity to drop male pollen onto female flowers, which in turn create cones with many seeds inside. The coastal redwood cone itself is small in comparison to other conifers, and the seeds of the giants are very small, with anywhere from 150 to 250 seeds found inside. In the fall, cones open and drop the seeds. During the early twentieth century, large redwood lumber mill companies would collect seeds to plant in their greenhouses to later be planted in logged-over regions. This work began in 1907 in Fort Bragg, California. Sixteen years later, the *Santa Ana Register* noted that The Pacific Lumber Company "has a nursery of 500,000 trees at Scotia." Many of the seeds had been collected from trees now protected near Dyerville. Additionally, seeds were collected by biologists for research. CCC workers, for example, were tasked with finding one hundred pounds of redwood seeds for biologists at U.C. Berkeley in the 1930s. Currently, the Save the Redwoods League is working with state and national parks to plant trees to help recover logged-over lands. Reforestation takes advantage of the redwood being one of the fastest-growing conifers. Records show that redwoods can, under ideal conditions, grow up to two feet per year. Although floods can be devastating, silt deposited also provides natural sites for seeds to sprout.

Redwood needles, like its flowers, also come in two distinct styles, both adapted to different needs of the tree. Researcher Alana Chin notes that the two types of needles "helps the trees adapt to both wet and dry conditions,"[15] which in turn may help the tree survive climate changes. Wide, flat needles are found lower on the tree. A redwood can have more than 100 million needles. These multipurpose leaves collect water, absorb it into the needles and let it drop on the forest below, watering its roots. The needles can do this with fog, helping the trees survive the long, dry summers of Northern California. Needles found near the top of the tree resemble the needles of the *Sequoia gigantea*. More like the spines of a cactus, these needles are very small and close together, thus reducing the amount of water lost to the atmosphere. Both types of needles have chlorophyll and will absorb water, but one keeps the tree moist, while the other reduces the amount of water lost near the tops of the trees. This adaptation is another clue to the long lives of the trees.

Beyond living a long time, redwoods are also capable of "cloning" themselves—growing from root sprouts near the base of the tree. This ability, along with the thick bark, gives the trees their scientific name, *Sempervirens*. Root sprouts can be easily seen throughout the forest. In the center of a group of trees in a circle is a large pit, where the original tree grew. In logged-over areas, stumps can be surrounded by small trees. Burlington campground in Humboldt Redwoods State Park was logged in the 1910s and '20s and features many of these cloned trees, growing around the original stump. These sprouts are genetically identical to the original tree. More recently, scientists have cloned trees that were identified as fast growing and "champion trees."

Further helping the redwoods to be "ever living" is their thick bark. The tough, fibrous bark can be up to two feet thick and is naturally fire resistant. There are few volatile oils or resins. Further, the bark's low pH or acidity keeps weeds away from the tree. According the SRL, "The bark also holds large quantities of water." The bark thus stores water from rain events for the tree to use during the dry summer months. The xylem layer, just beneath the bark, also has water in it. Old-time loggers described the water that came out of the bark and xylem as a shower. The bark is deeply furrowed, guiding water to the roots. Similar to the needles of the tree, the bark can absorb

The narrow needles found near the top of the *Sequoia sempervirens* are similar to those found on the *Sequoiadendron giganteum*. *Carol Russell.*

water from fog and mist and transfer that moisture to the xylem. In a 2020 study by John-Pascal Berrill et al., he and his team determined that the thick bark also helps protect the tree in more arid conditions, on the southern fringes of the tree's range and on hillsides. The bark on a tree also varies in thickness from the base to higher on the tree. Although fire resistant, the bark can be broached by a hot fire, leaving behind a tree with a hollow base, often referred to as a "goose-pen," but the tree continues to grow. In fact, the bark will begin to cover over the burned region, protecting the inner layers of wood. After logging of the trees began in earnest in the 1850s, various uses for the bark were tried. For example, the bark was used as an insulation material in schools and other buildings in the early twentieth century. It was also experimented with during World War II for use as blankets.

The wood is naturally insect repelling and is resistant to termites. The wood's outer layer is where the tree transports nutrients and water. The wood in the interior is more for stability for the tree. A final attribute of the wood, its ability to split easily, led to an entire industry based on the friability of redwood. The split products industry and its impact on the trees led SRL founder Grant Merriam to write, "It is scarcely necessary to dwell on the crime involved in the destruction of the oldest and tallest trees on earth. The cutting of a sequoia for grape stakes or railroad ties is like breaking up one's grandfather's clock for kindling to save the trouble of splitting logs at the woodpile or lighting one's pipe with a Greek manuscript to save the trouble of reaching for the matches."

The Native Americans who lived along the Northern California coastline were the first humans to utilize the redwoods. In what is now Humboldt County, there were thirteen distinct tribes. These first peoples, along with the Tolowas, found in current Del Norte County, used redwood in multiple ways. These tribes used the fallen redwood trees to extract planks to build their houses. The Tolowas built semi-subterranean homes, with circular entrances and plank roofs and sides. This style was replicated by the Yuroks and Wiyots. The Sinkyones and Nongatls built homes that were more conical but still used redwood. Redwood roots were used in basketry. Redwood logs were used to make dugout canoes similar to those used by other tribes along the Pacific Northwest. Fire was used to burn out sections of the boat, and the burnt sections were scraped out. A heart and lungs were also carved into the tree to respect the life of the tree. According to Albert Elasser in the *California Handbook of Native Americans*, the dugout canoe was used as far south as the mouth of South Fork of the Eel River. The Nongatls, who lived along the Van Duzen River, near present-day Grizzly Creek, also used the redwoods to make dugout canoes.[16] First Peoples living farther south used reed mats or rafts.

When Spanish explorers began to settle in central California in the 1760s, they were the first Europeans to encounter the redwoods. They

Left: A chopper making an undercut illustrates the thick redwood bark; two men could take several days to chop through the dense bark. *FDM*.

Below: Drawn by a soldier at Fort Humboldt in the 1850s, this is one of the earliest images of the mills around Humboldt Bay. *CPHLSC*.

found redwoods to be too large to mill easily or cut down for use. When they did, their mills were powered by hand, with one person in a pit below the log and another above, pulling manually on a saw. Thus redwoods were mostly untouched when gold was discovered in 1848. The U.S. Census Bureau noted, "News of the discovery of gold in California reached the eastern United States by August 1848. President James Polk confirmed the discovery in an address to Congress on December 5, 1850....Between 1850 and 1860, California's population grew from 92,597 to 379,994—a 310 percent increase!" This dramatic escalation in population meant that California became a state in 1850 and created a huge demand for timber to build houses and businesses for new residents.

Settlements begin in 1850 around Humboldt Bay. These early residents of Eureka and Union, now known as Arcata, also found redwoods difficult to log and mill. During these first years of settlement, lumber was actually imported into the area, as the nearby trees could not be harvested. One of the first mills in Humboldt, near the mouth of Little River, the Luffelholz mill, north of Arcata, actually milled Douglas fir trees. The issue of a source

Oxen hauled logs across a skid road, made of small logs, to mills around Humboldt Bay from Ryan Slough in this 1880s image. *CPHLSC.*

for power in the mills was solved in 1852 when James Ryan started a mill along the bay, according to Jerry Rhode in a 2012 historical survey of the McKay Tract. To power the mill, Ryan steered "the side-wheel steamship *Santa Clara* onto the Eureka shoreline at the foot of D Street." Ryan's mill was "the first really successful mill in the Humboldt Bay region." While the problem of powering a mill was resolved, many more issues had to be solved before redwood logging began in earnest in the 1870s.

Technological challenges of felling redwood were solved by changes in steel manufacturing occurring due to needing stronger cannons during the Civil War. Sturdier axe steel meant that choppers could more easily cut through the trees' fibrous bark. Above the butt swell of the tree, loggers discovered not only that the bark was thinner but also that the wood was easier to chop. Thus, scaffolding or staging boards, sometimes called spring boards, were built up and around the base of the tree. While standing on these metal-tipped boards, placed in the tree, two choppers began making the undercut. After chopping out the undercut, the men moved to the opposite side of the tree. There they used the two-man crosscut saw, often referred to by loggers as a "misery whip," to finish cutting the tree down. The loggers would use a "gunning" stick to determine where a tree would fall. To avoid the tree shattering when it fell, men built a "bed" of branches, dirt and other debris to cushion the tree. The reiterated branches of the crown were always a danger to watch for, as well as falling branches from the tree being logged, gaining them the grim but accurate moniker of "widow-makers."

Once a tree was on the ground, loggers discovered that stripping the bark from the tree allowed it to be more easily moved. Peelers, using long steel rods, pried and peeled the bark off, leaving the bark in the woods. The long logs were also sawn into manageable lengths. To solve the issue of hauling the logs to a mill, mills were often built near the site where the trees were being felled, such as the Jolly Giant mill, operated by Noah Falk. Located on the site of current Cal Poly Humboldt, the mill was close to large stands of redwoods. As trees near the mill were cut down, oxen, mules or horses were used to pull long "trains" of logs to the mills. The peeled logs slid along a skid road of smaller logs "greased" with water. While some logs were floated to the mills, this was more of a rarity, as the Eel River would take the logs farther south of Eureka and the smaller creeks around the bay were not suitable for logs to be floated to the mills. However, some companies did float logs in Humboldt Bay to the various mills.

Animals were limited in how far and how many logs they could pull in a day. In 1887, an exceptionally large load of seven logs was yarded by a five-yoke of oxen under the guidance of bull puncher A.A. Marks. Normal loads were pulled by three to four pairs of oxen or mules, limiting output of woods' crews. This changed with the arrival of the steam donkey in the woods. Invented by Bay Mill co-owner John Dolbeer, the steam engine allowed logs to be pulled a longer distance. Using an auxiliary steam engine from a ship, known as a donkey engine because it produced less power than the main engines, the upright steam donkey soon became a staple in the woods. Uses included pulling logs, loading railroad cars that replaced the oxen and even moving itself through the woods. Dolbeer also invented a locomotive engine that could pull and push a load of logs. Railroads became important to the lumber industry as the tall timber that had once grown around Humboldt Bay was cut down, replaced with homes and businesses. The mill owners found trains necessary to access trees growing farther away from Eureka mills.

Railroads spread out from the harbor at Eureka, and mills soon followed. In the 1880s, mills were started south of Humboldt Bay at Scotia and north in Del Norte County. Advertising redwood lumber attributes helped increase sales. In addition to being used to build houses, boardwalks and curbs were being built in San Francisco and Sacramento with redwood, according to the specifications for projects. In 1897, the Redwood Logging Association published "Souvenir of the Redwood Lumber Industry." In addition to touting the use of the straight grain of the redwood for building houses, the booklet also noted that redwood lumber was being used to build coffins, "for which [the wood] is sawed in a special way so that the grain is vertical. When this has been prepared, grained and polished in a proper manner, he must be little less than an expert who is not deceived into believing it genuine rosewood or mahogany." The wood was also being used to make doors and mouldings for doors and ceilings, as well as brackets. According to logging companies, redwood also was being used to make furniture, "mantels, sideboards, desks, counters, fancy table tops, book cases, interior finish of cars, fine paneled bedsteads, and all kinds of massive furniture, newell posts, banisters, grille work…no wood is so easily worked, or will remain so perfectly or securely in place with shrinking or swelling as redwood." Ironically, as dry redwood burns very quickly, the book also describes the wood as being fire resistant, which is true only for wet wood. The text further touts redwoods as making for a durable railroad tie. Redwood tanks and pipers were other commodities that could be made from the redwood, along with shingles for the exterior of houses. The efforts of the lumber companies were successful, and demand rose for more

Steam donkeys required a smaller crew to operate than oxen teams and worked longer. Pictured machine is in the Pacific Lumber Larabee woods. *CPHLSC.*

redwood lumber. In 1891, according to *Memorial and Biographical History of Northern California*, the Excelsior Lumber Company was operating "day and night, sawing the gigantic logs. The operations are very interesting, many new devices being adopted to handle the enormous sticks."[17]

The rapid cutting of redwoods was viewed with alarm by concerned residents of the state and nation, who worried that the miles of redwood forests were being decimated. In 1879, U.S. Secretary of the Interior Carl Schurz advocated for preservation of California's redwood forests. The *Pacific Bee* reported in November of that year that Schurz recommended action, including "immediate steps by Congress to protect the redwood and big trees of California." Schurz's plan included the creation of two forty-six-thousand-acre parks, one in Northern California, presumably in the Humboldt and Mendocino region, and one farther south near Monterey.[18] That same year, U.S. Representative George Converse of Ohio introduced a bill into Congress authorizing President Hayes to

> *select from the United States Public land in California such tracts on which are growing either the redwood* [Sequoia semperviren], *or the big tree* [Sequoia gigantean], *or both that may deem proper no exceeding in aggregate two townships of land…withdraw them from settlement…to be set apart as public parks.…Each of these parks is to be under the exclusive control of the secretary of the Interior, who shall cause them to be surveyed and prescribe the regulations for their care and management.*[19]

Creation of these redwood parks would have greatly changed the redwood conservation movement, marking their preservation as a civic matter rather than becoming dependent on public-spirited conservationists and those who donated privately to preserve the trees for all. Ultimately, this was the course that was followed, as Schurz and Converse were unable to convince President Hayes and Congress of the need to save the trees. The preservation movement stalled but was not stopped, as interest in conservation and preservation continued to rise during the late Gilded Age as reformists began to point out many areas of concern in health and safety, as well as resource destruction. While various groups continued to urge for the preservation of the redwoods, by 1900, there were no longer any coastal redwood trees left in public lands, all the forests being owned privately by mill companies.[20]

By 1900, the mills around Humboldt Bay had consumed all the trees that were close to the bay. Mill owners had begun to look farther afield for

"Pond monkeys," log pond workers, push logs into Excelsior Mill, partly owned by Joseph Russ, located on Gunther's Island in Humboldt Bay. *CPHLSC.*

Schooner *Bertha Dolbeer* and the *Azalea* are tied up to the Carson and Dolbeer Bay Mill dock, loading with lumber. *CPHLSC.*

Loggers stand on logs on railcars, surrounded by burnt forest. After logging, the site was burned to remove undergrowth and the fallen branches. *CPHLSC.*

redwoods to supply their mills. The forests south of The Pacific Lumber Company at Scotia began to be sourced. The Pacific Lumber Company formed in 1869, but no lumbering operations began until 1886. That year, the company extended a rail line north to Alton to connect to the Eel River and Eureka Railroad, completed the previous year. The mill was built by John Vance and William Carson, and its owners profited by being able to haul logs to their mills, as well as lumber for The Pacific Lumber Company. The mills had also changed from being located near the trees they milled to being larger operations with logs brought to them by rail. A greater change to logging came with the arrival of Andrew Hammond in the redwood lumber business. Hammond was a follower of the dictates of other magnates of the Gilded Age—such as Andrew Carnegie and John Rockefeller—devoted to finding ways to cut costs to increase his profits. To that end, he ensured control of all aspects of his operations, from raising chickens and pigs to feeding his men to where he sold lumber, in his own lumberyards in the San Francisco and Los Angeles regions. He also dramatically changed logging practices that had held sway since the 1850s. Hammond decided that not logging in the wintertime was not a financially sound practice and commenced logging year-round, even in the rainy season. This way he guaranteed a steady supply of logs to his mills.

Railroads connected woods operations to mills, and loggers lived in camps near the sites that were being logged. By 1921, Hammond had control of eighty-seven thousand acres of forestland. Other local mill operators quickly followed suit. The results were devastating to the redwoods, the surrounding hills and creeks. In addition to allowing more trees to be cut, winter rains washed away topsoil, leaving wide gullies behind. Near Trinidad, California, in the 1920s, wildfires raged several times, destroying acres of forestland. Catastrophic forest fires further added to damage being done to the fragile giants. Some of the fires were intentionally started, since a common practice was to burn the slash and debris left from logging. Branches, bark and tree tops, as well as smaller trees, were all destroyed, which resulted "in the loss of a full third of the potential timber."[21]

The turn of the century was a period of highs and lows for the preservation of the redwoods. Phoebe Hearst and others, including photographer A.P. Hill, raised funds to preserve what is now Big Basin Redwoods State Park near Santa Cruz. Nearly four thousand acres of trees were purchased in 1902 through the combined efforts of members of the Sempervirens Club and the state legislature. The *Oakland Tribune* praised the work of the Oakland Chapter of the Daughters of the American Revolution

Andrew Hammond purchased the Vance Mill at Samoa in 1903, instituting changes in woods and mill operations causing rapid depletion of redwood forests. *CPHLSC.*

for joining with the Sempervirens Club to advocate for preservation of the redwoods in the Big Basin area. The club's brochure was quoted in the paper:

> *The redwood is geologically speaking, one of the oldest trees in existence, tracing its descent from the Pliocene or period before the Ice Age. The "Big Basin" forest is therefore of great interest to science, as containing the oldest specimens of plant life known....At the present rate of destruction this forest—the growth of many centuries, will be wiped out in five years. Immediate action must be taken to preserve it.[22]*

The efforts were supported in 1908 when Congressmen William Kent donated what is now Muir Woods to the federal government to honor John Muir.[23]

Residents of Humboldt County were also influenced by the national reform fervor, aware of diminishing stands of redwoods near the bay. One of the earliest attempts in Humboldt County to preserve the redwoods was started in Humboldt by concerned residents in 1915. Near the town of Fortuna was a beautiful grove of redwoods, known as Carson Woods, used frequently as a picnic grounds. For example, the Woodsmen of the World held its annual meetings at the site in 1907, and the Oddfellows had their annual picnic at the 2,200-acre parcel in 1916. That same year, a group of newspapermen from the San Francisco Bay Area traveled by rail to Humboldt to explore the region. One of their stops was Carson Woods, described by editor of the *Concord Transcript* Miss Catherine Burke as "fascinating in their grandeur, being a vast forest of the loftiest monarchs of nature that the eye ever behold."[24] Burke also noted that the regions' redwoods gave "an idea of the wonderful timber wealth that has made this section famous." Thus, it was in this juxtaposition of forest conservation and the wealth the trees represented that a group of concerned citizens met in Ferndale in 1915. The group comprised residents from Eureka, Arcata and Fortuna. The organizer of the meeting was E.W. Haight, of Fortuna, part owner of the Williams Creek Mill Company. Very active in the community, he served on the school board and participated in many organizations. The gathered residents were in agreement of the need to preserve the grove and were inspired to start raising funds to purchase the grove. At the meeting, it was noted that "Congressmen [William] Kent has promised to give $25,000 toward the purchase of a redwood park in this county, and has also expressed his belief that among his associates he

THAVIUS BAND. CARSON WOODS
FORTUNA CAL (BOW. 47)

The Thavius Band poses in front of a large redwood in Carson Woods. This grove was logged by Holmes Eureka in the 1920s. *CPHLSC.*

can raise at least another $25,000 and perhaps $75,000."[25] Unfortunately for residents of the county, world events overtook the attempts to preserve Carson Woods. With the end of World War I and the following influenza pandemic, along with the increased demand for lumber, owners of the tract decided to log it. In 1922, Holmes-Eureka Lumber Company purchased the grove, further agreeing to extend several Fortuna streets. The editor of the *Fortuna Advance*, who had urged preservation of Carson Woods, bemoaned, "Carson Woods with its centuries old giants is doomed.… Carson Woods which should have perpetuated the memory of a grand old gentleman [William Carson], will in a few short months be a hideous sight of charred stumps, revolting to the lover of nature."[26]

Humboldt County residents continued to support efforts to preserve the tall trees. In 1920, the *Ferndale Enterprise* devoted its February 27 edition to the cause of the newly formed Save the Redwoods League. Editor and proprietor Herbert Briggs wrote, "The Redwood has been termed the masterpiece of Nature's handiwork. A mature tree is the finished creation of centuries of summer's sunshine and winter's rain; to the lover of a nature an inspiration and an object of reverence." Capturing the reform-minded spirit of the time, he continued: "This noble creation is threatened with extermination by the ruthless hand of commercialism." He saluted those who created the Save the Redwoods League, "men and women, not alone in the shadow of the mighty forests but from all parts of the land." He concluded, "*The Enterprise* is proud to aid in the fight to the extent of its power and gladly uses the support of its columns today to men and women of Ferndale who are devoting themselves unselfishly to the cause." The paper included a sermon by Reverend Douglass of the Ferndale Congregational Church on the need to preserve the redwoods. Douglass urged immediate action on part of concerned residents to protect the trees. Also included in the paper were poems by local residents Georgia Williams, daughter of Excelsior mill owner Joseph Russ, and Amy Hunter. The paper noted that the Women's Save the Redwoods League of Humboldt County was seeking pictures of the redwoods to help advertise their plight. The paper further noted that while the State of California was working on bond issues to purchase some twenty thousand acres of redwood lands, "two of Humboldt's patriotic women, Mrs. Sarah J. Perrott and Mrs. H.W. McClellan have given a splendid example of their unselfish interest in the welfare of others by generously donating valuable timber land with the proposed park area."[27] The efforts of the *Ferndale Enterprise* and Reverend Douglass were also supported by Zipporah Russ, a longtime

Ferndale resident who, three years later, would donate land near Orick, forming the genesis of present-day Prairie Creek Redwoods State Park.

Thus, the preservation movements of the early 1900s were confronted and often stymied due to a greatly increased demand for lumber caused by one of the largest natural disasters to rock California since the arrival of Euro-Americans in the 1770s. The 1906 earthquake and fire in the San Francisco Bay region created a huge demand for lumber. Mills began operating two and sometimes three shifts to keep up with the need to rebuild homes and businesses. Another demand for lumber came with the rise of the Craftsman bungalow house, with its demand for shingles for siding as well as the roof. Combined, the demand for redwood became even greater. Shipping redwood lumber to markets as well as accessing timber farther from the mills around Humboldt Bay became of increased concern to mill owners.

Starting in 1907, negotiations began to connect the railroad that terminated at Willits with The Pacific Lumber Company's line that extended to Shively, a distance of some one hundred miles. The San Luis Obispo *Morning Tribune* reported that year that "it is estimated that there are about 400,000,000 feet of standing redwood timber at the present time, or enough to keep all the saw mills constantly at work for the next 100 years. On or near Humboldt Bay there are nine large saw mills and many shingle mills in operation. And thus far the only outlet for this lumber has been by vessels out of Humboldt Bay."[28] The completion of the Northwestern Pacific Railroad in 1914, connecting Humboldt County to the markets of California, also opened new areas for logging. The Pacific Lumber Company had already created a camp near the community of Shively, but now the large trees along the South Fork of the Eel River were accessible to the railroad and waiting to be harvested. The area known as Holmes Flat was logged three times by the Holmes-Eureka company with the building of the railroad. Another grove, Sonoma Flat, perceived by some to be a stand of trees to rival what is now Founder's Grove, was also logged after the railroad came through the region. In 1914, San Francisco mayor James Rolph was filmed aboard the "Redwood Empire Special," a special train with 117 cars loaded with 3 million feet of redwood lumber destined for twenty-one different states. The railroad led to another boom in the logging industry in the 1920s, following World War I.

As with technology developed during the Civil War, technological advances made during World War I also made their way to the woods. The large two-handed misery whips used to saw the logs into manageable lengths were replaced with large dragsaws allowing two men to more quickly

A logger uses a dragsaw; although large, bulky and unwieldly, the new machine greatly reduced the time needed to log a tree. *CPHLSC.*

saw the logs in the woods. In 1920, Edward Morris of Willits reported to the *Timberman* that he had used the new tool to complete an order for fifty thousand railroad ties. He noted that the dragsaws are of "great value as [redwood] is springy and difficult for crews to pull ordinary saws through."[29] Another technology affecting redwood logging was the advent of the tractor crawler, informally known as bull dozers or "Cats" after the Caterpillar company began manufacturing the crawlers. The machine used treads developed for tanks during World War I. The Cats also helped cut costs, as they did not require the crew the old steam donkeys had utilized. Using an arch, the dozers replaced the donkey as the tool of choice to bring the logs to a landing, causing further damage to the forest undergrowth.

Although automobiles had been used on Humboldt roads since the turn of the century, the end of the war brought an interest in building highways to accommodate vehicles, better than the previous wagon roads. Starting in the late 1910s construction began of what was to become the Redwood Highway, U.S. 101. Road construction exposed the fragile roots of the redwood, often killing the trees. Other practices such as dumping soil on top of the roots was also damaging to the trees. The stage was set then in

A car is parked beside Bolling Grove, the first grove preserved by the Save the Redwoods League in 1921. *Smithsonian Institution Archives, #SIA2015-003193.*

1917, when the future founders of the Save the Redwoods League headed north from San Francisco at the behest of Stephen Mather, first director of the National Park Service, to find out for themselves the status of the tall trees. What they found was alarming. The situation was grim, from the standpoint of preservation of the forests. A 1919 U.S. Forest Service report estimated that the entire redwood belt from Monterey to Del Norte County was estimated to be 1,406,393 acres prior to logging. In 1922, the SRL found "the remaining stand of virgin redwood timber is…951,000 acres, or a little less than a million. Forest Service figures that this area is being cut over at the rate of 6,500 acres per year."[30] The SRL worked hard to raise money, sharing images showing the destruction of the redwood groves. Stimulating the need to preserve the trees were changes in logging methods, including logging year-round, leaving devastated areas behind. The SRL was able to preserve its first grove in 1921 with money donated by the family of Colonel Raynal Bolling. Soon, more groves along the Redwood Highway were purchased and preserved, becoming the first of the redwood state parks, Humboldt Redwoods State Park.

Chapter 2

HUMBOLDT REDWOODS
STATE PARKS

Appropriately enough, the story of the formation of the Save the Redwoods League and Humboldt Redwoods State Park begins with a camping trip. In the summer of 1917, members of the Bohemian Club, a group founded in 1872 in San Francisco for journalists, met at the Bohemian Grove of Redwoods near Guerneville on the Russian River. Members included alumni and professors from Berkeley as well as wealthy businessmen. The club owned the grove, as members had a wide range of interests. That year, attendees included Horace Albright, assistant to Stephen Mather, the first director of the National Park Service. Albright was hoping that by attending the camp he could encourage the members to support the national park movement, including creation of a national redwood park.

Also in attendance were Henry Fairfield Osborn from the American Museum of Natural History and Madison Grant, a lawyer and zoologist. According to Joseph Engbeck in *Saving the North-Coast Redwoods*, Grant was interested in the national parks movement. The two friends planned a trip that summer, traveling to Crater Lake, Mount Rainier and Yellowstone National Parks. They were also trying to convince University of California professor of paleontology John C. Merriam to join them. Discussions at the Bohemian Grove that summer included highway construction and how improved roads would allow access to parks. The men at the grove thought that linking the national park movement to the improved highways program would be a useful idea. Redwood preservation was a hot topic that summer, as in May of that year Governor Stephens signed a bill appropriating

"150,000 for the purchase of additional land for Redwood Park in Big Basin in Santa Cruz County."[31] The bill, reported the *Sacramento Bee*, "provided the means of preserving what had been declared to be the finest redwood forest in the United States, outside of that already in the park." Preservation of the Big Basin trees had been timely as well, as a sawmill had been planned to be erected shortly for milling the forest.

John C. Merriam, Madison Grant and Fairfield Osborn left the Russian River area late in July, heading for Humboldt County. The journey took several days to accomplish, as the only reliable road at the time was what is now Highway 1, along the Sonoma and Mendocino coast. On their way, the men passed many large redwood mills, including those at Little River, Casper and Fort Bragg. They also saw the impact of fifty years of redwood logging in this region. The Fort Bragg mill alone had a capacity for sawing 120,000 board feet per day. All the redwood trees along the coast were privately owned by eleven lumber companies. Much of the original redwood forest had been logged or was in the process of being cut. Thus, when the men arrived along the South Fork of the Eel River, they clearly understood the logging threat, seeing the devastated stumps and debris left behind. The three were transfixed by the uniqueness of the redwoods they found near the small community of Dyerville.

In 1928, Merriam described this first trip to see the redwoods along the South Fork and how the redwoods affected him and his fellow travelers. His descriptions capture the awe they felt when they first saw these spectacular groves as they drove along Bull Creek, through what is now Rockefeller Forest:

Suddenly we swung from the highway, dropping down a steep slope into primeval redwood timber. The car quieted as its wheels rolled over the leafy carpet. The road soon ended in a trail, and the party proceeded on foot.

As we advanced, the arches of foliage narrowed above us, and shade deepened into twilight. Between close-set trunks one looked through windows framed in shadow often darkening till all detail disappeared. Here and there behind these openings was a distant aisle in which faint touches of sun upon the shaft of a young tree brought out its red-brown glow. Through other reaches vision was lost in failing light. Like pillars of a temple, the giant columns spaced themselves with mutual support, producing unity and not mere symmetry. The men of the company who all their lives had known great forests, bared their heads in this presence. Ponderous strength, an almost infinite variety in expression of light and shade and color, and a perspective with marvelously changing depth composed a scene such as

The redwoods along Bull Creek exemplify John Merriam's description, standing "like pillars of a temple, the giant columns...producing unity." *CPHLSC.*

canvas has yet to receive....We realized that the mysterious influence of this grove arose not alone from magnitude, or from beauty of light filling deep spaces. It was as if in these trees the flow of years were held in eddies, and one saw together past and present. The element of time pervaded the forest with an influence more subtle than light with that to the mind was not less real.[32]

The impact of the grove was powerful, leading them to implement a campaign that continues to this day to preserve, to protect and to educate about the redwoods.

The men continued to explore in the region, and while they were thrilled by the redwoods, they were concerned with damage being done by both road construction and logging. As mentioned, while the railroad had recently been completed, the trees remained too large to be easily handled to take to the mills and were instead being cut into split products, such as shingles, grapestakes and railroad ties. In the three miles between Dyerville and Weott, there were several such operations, and in Weott, or McKee's Mill as it was known at the time, there was a much larger mill. In 1919, Madison Grant wrote in an article for the *New York Zoological Society Magazine* noting that the split products industry was one of the greatest threats to the tall trees. Based on their ability to be easily split, the trees were "doomed to the ignoble fate of being riven for railroad ties, for shakes or shingles, and perhaps worst of all, for grapestakes." Given the immediate threats to these groves of redwoods, the men determined to create an organization devoted to the preservation of the redwoods. They also drafted a letter to the governor of California, William Stephens, calling for immediate action to stop logging of these groves along the South Fork of the Eel.

Grant and Osborn wrote, in part, "I express a very strong conviction that this stretch of forest should be preserved for the benefit of the people of the state, through reservation as a state park."[33] In addition to having easy access to the nascent Highway 101, the men believed that it would make a good campground; the park would be considered the "most popular acts of the administration of the State."[34] Further, they felt that "the matter may commend itself to your judgement and the means of making this glorious forest secure for all times for the people may be found."[35] While John Merriam had not signed the letter, he wrote one to the chairman of the California Highway Commission, Charles Stern, advocating for considering the natural scenic roadways while highways were built. Unfortunately, Merriam's letter did not receive attention, and the highway commission

The highway commission sold the road edges to logging companies to harvest, including for split products, that could be hauled by truck. *HRIA.*

continued to sell rights to the trees along the state right-of-way, which led to the need for SRL and the state to repurchase groves along the roadside to protect them from being logged.

With their return to San Francisco, the men's efforts began in earnest. With an initial donation of $100, the Save the Redwoods League was formed in 1918. In the summer of 1919, the first official meeting for the group was held, and they determined the league goals:

- To secure the finest and most available tract of redwood timber as a national park;
- To secure a strip 300 yards wide or other suitable width along each side of the highway as state park; and
- To obtain by private gifts such other fine tracts of land as may be recommended by a committee appointed to make a thorough study of the redwood situation.[36]

The men also gained support from other organizations, such as the Sempervirens League and the General Federation of Women Clubs. One of the new association's first acts was to contact groups and individuals they thought would be interested, including those teaching at western universities and members of the Sierra Club. Aware of the tourism potential, they also contacted automobile clubs and proponents of the good roads movement. Their letter writing campaign was successful, and by the end of 1920, membership exceeded four thousand. Members included those involved in the logging industry, as many felt that these outstanding groves should be preserved.

Grant and other league members also directed national attention to the threat presented to redwoods from logging. Grant made many nationwide appeals for support, writing articles printed in newspapers across the United States and the world urging preservation of the redwoods. In 1919, Madison Grant wrote an article in the *New York Zoological Society Magazine*, an organization for which he served as secretary, about the need to preserve the redwoods. He advocated for the formation of a national park to protect the trees. Grant pointed out to readers that "at the present rate of destruction the old stand of forests in the United States will be cut over the next sixty years. It will not last sixty years because the new and efficient methods of logging by machinery."[37] After explaining the uniqueness of the redwood forest and reiterating the threat to the trees, he pointed out the imminent need to preserve the trees along the South Fork of the Eel and Bull Creek:

> *Four great forests stand out prominently: They are the groves along the South Fork of the Eel River and the west bank of the main Eel culminating in the Bull Creek Flat and the Dyerville Flat; the immense Redwood Creek grove; the Klamath River groves and the Smith River groves in Del Norte County. Each has its peculiar beauty and it is difficult to choose among them, but it is the trees of Humboldt which at the present are most in peril.*[38]

Grant included the results of a trip in 1919 to survey the redwoods. He observed that the majority of redwood forests in Mendocino had been logged. Further, the first large grove in Humboldt County, in what is now Richardson Grove, was threatened because the highway commission planned on having the highway right-of-way logged. Grant further listed areas being logged, for split products, and where potential groves should be purchased. He noted in regards to Bull Creek Flats that both The Pacific Lumber Company and Metropolitan Lumber Company were principal land owners and that "the officials of both these companies expressed their sympathy with the park project as far as it relates to Bull Creek Flat."[39] Grant also noted that the flat was "said to contain one enormous tree, possibly the largest Redwood and the tallest tree in the world."[40] Grant ended his description with the need to preserve the forests in national, state and county parks by noting that "the salvation of these great trees probably will depend on two factors just entering into active political life, one the automobilists and the other, the women voters." Both groups would be important to the preservation of the redwoods, as would a third group, veterans.

During the survey trip in 1919, Madison Grant and Stephen Mather also traveled to Eureka to discuss the need to preserve the redwoods along Bull Creek with interested members of the public. Their gathering was well attended, with Grant urging gathered participants to form their own Save the Redwoods League. This admonition found fertile ground; the following day, Laura Perrott Mahan formed the Women's Save the Redwoods League of Humboldt County. The first meeting was held on September 20, 1919, at the Eureka City Hall Council Chambers. The *Humboldt Beacon* noted that "all women of the county who are interested in the movement to save the big trees are invited to be present."[41] The paper reported in August that "Mrs. R.R. Smith was selected vice-chairman for the Save the Redwoods League for the Fortuna District." At the gathering, "held by the campaign committee of the League," there was "a very enthusiastic meeting with a number of the women present who are anxious to do whatever they can to save the giants of the forests of Humboldt."[42] The principal speaker at the meeting was Mrs. A.J. Monroe. The paper explained that "the whole county was to be organized as one league and a chairman from each the different sections of the county will represent their district at the general meetings."[43] A similar organizational meeting was led by Monroe in Ferndale. The *Ferndale Enterprise* observed that "all ladies of this community are urged to attend and help the good work."[44]

The Women's Save the Redwoods League of Humboldt County was a very active organization. Members of the Ferndale branch, in October 1919, had a "table at the Citizen's Furniture Co.'s store in Ferndale every afternoon…and hope[d] to sign up every woman in the community as a member of this organization which is playing such a vital part in the movement to preserve Humboldt's giant Sequoias." Committee members Mrs. D.A. Francis, Mrs. L.C. Ericcsen and Mrs. F.M. Bruner hoped that "every woman in Ferndale and vicinity will join, pay the fifty cents dues and help give the rest of the county a splendid report of Ferndale's deep interest in saving the Redwoods."[45] The following year, in February, the Women's Save the Redwoods League solicited images of the redwoods for Dr. John Merriam to use in magazines and publications. Desired were "exceptionally beautiful pictures of the big trees."[46] Additionally, members planned a photographic trip with a photographer, possibly Emma Bell Richart

Right: Laura Perrott Mahan helped form the Women's Save the Redwoods League, actively working to preserve the redwoods. *HHS*.

Below: The Women's Save the Redwoods League was active in soliciting donations and encouraging landowners to donate lands to the SRL. *HHS*.

Freeman, whose images were used in Madison Grant's article in the *New York Zoological Society Bulletin* in September 1919. Freeman was a Humboldt County photographer, who along with her husband, Edwin Freeman, operated Freeman Art Company. Both took many images of the redwoods that were often used in postcards. After Edwin and Emma divorced in 1915, Edwin went on to manage Richardson Grove, both for Henry Devoy and later for the state park system. During this time, he took many images of that area. Emma continued to take pictures of the redwoods, and she was also renowned for her staged studio photography of local Native Americans.

Members of the Women's Save the Redwoods League wrote their own articles about the need to preserve the redwoods. Edna Hildebrandt Putnam of Oakland wrote an article for the General Federation of Women's Clubs, also published in the August 1920 *Travel* magazine. Putnam traveled to the redwoods along the South Fork the previous year after hearing Madison Grant speak about the plight of the redwoods. She was amazed by the trees but shocked by the devastation wrought by both logging practices and highway construction. She observed:

> [W]e tramped about among the wreckage of the two sawmills and various tie camps. It hadn't been pleasant. The colonnade of stately old trees towering two and three hundred feet toward heaven had given place to piles of grape stakes, telegraph poles and railroad ties. And, as if to add to the atmosphere of desolation the piles of brush and debris had been burned over in order that the massive trunks of the fallen monarchs might be managed more easily.[47]

Perhaps her most convincing argument for the preservation of the redwoods stemmed from her caption of one of the images used in the book:

> The redwood realm has been lumbering country for fifty years and will continue for the next fifty. The "Save the Redwoods" campaign in no way seeks to interfere with this legitimate and necessary business but to restrict it to necessity and to save the great trees directly bordering the highway and a representation forest tract to remind future generations of the marvel God wrought in the great redwood forests that will then have vanished forever. Sections of the redwood forests now resemble the devastated areas of France. Shall we countenance in California that which we have condemned in France?[48]

Putnam's concerns about the redwood's devastation were based on sights like those found at Pacific Lumber Company's Camp A operations. *CPHLSC.*

Putnam noted that the only redwood lands that had been donated were those by two widows, Mrs. Sarah Perrott and Mrs. Martha McClellan of Eureka. Both women were pioneers of the county. Sarah had traveled to California over the plains when she was seven, according to her obituary.[49] She married William Perrott in 1864, moving to Humboldt shortly after. The Perrotts settled near Loleta, operating a dairy farm. Martha Cook McClellan (whose family had immigrated to California from Iowa) and her husband, Hugh, married in 1872. Hugh McClellan came to California in 1857, first helping his brother in Crescent City. He became partners in a sheep ranch east of Bridgeville in the 1870s. He ultimately operated a sheep ranch covering 11,000 acres. The couple lived in Eureka after 1881, where McClellan was a board member for the Humboldt Woolen Mill. The donation of 160 acres was made by both Mrs. McClellan and her two daughters, Mrs. James L. Fraser and Mrs. Hugh A. Graham, in 1919.[50] The women donated lands along the South Fork of the Eel. Both women would have been inspired to give their holdings by the Women's Save the Redwoods League. Perrott was also the mother of Laura Perrott Mahan and was well informed about the redwoods.

Colonel Raynal C. Bolling was the highest-ranking aviation officer killed in World War I. His family felt that a grove of redwoods was a worthy memorial. *Library of Congress.*

The Save the Redwoods League was able to begin purchasing back some of the right-of-ways sold by the highway commission and, with lands donated, made a start at preserving the redwoods. However, Grant and the other members were aware of how slow the federal government worked and, therefore, the need for immediate action. In 1920, SRL was incorporated as a nonprofit organization. Due to its continuing solicitation of funds and a generous donation from the Bolling family, it was able to purchase its first grove along the South Fork of the Eel. The Bolling family also helped by advertising for a grove in the lumber industry magazine *The Timberman.* Colonel Raynal C. Bolling, a native of Hot Springs, Arkansas, was the first high-ranking U.S. officer killed in World War I. Bolling was interested in aviation, becoming a pilot in 1915. He created "the first flying unit in what became the Air National Guard. Bolling was mustered into federal service and became a Reserve Military Aviator. On May 26, 1917, he stood up the 1st Reserve Aero Squadron—the first-ever in the Army Reserve." Promoted by General Pershing to colonel, "he was picked to run Air Service, US II Corps. On March 26, 1918, Bolling and his driver were inspecting his zone of operation at the front when they were attacked by German soldiers. Bolling was shot and killed. His remains were never recovered."[51] Bolling tried to save his driver's life before he, too, was hit. Bolling's bravery was recognized by the army with an air force base in Washington, D.C., being named for him. He was also remembered by his family with the grove. The *San Bernardino Daily Sun* reported on August 14, 1921, that "such a monument will grow in grandeur and beauty from year to year while monuments of stone will disappear and that which they commemorate be forgotten." In February 1921, the *Oxnard Press Courier* described Bolling Grove as "situated at the junction of Elk Creek and the

Dignitaries from the SRL, state and local officials gathered for the first dedication of a memorial grove in 1921 at Bolling Grove. *HRIA.*

South Fork of the Eel River, about 45 miles from Eureka, California, in the heart of the most representative areas of Sequoia Sempervirens, or redwoods. Through it passes the new state highway. It is situated at a bend of the South Fork of the Eel River and commands a striking vista of the river and the surrounding redwood region." The grove was about forty acres in size, on both sides of the highway and on either side of Elk Creek near its mouth.

The actual dedication of the grove occurred on August 1921. The *Humboldt Standard* reported that nearly 350 people gathered at the grove for the dedication. Dignitaries from Eureka picked up those traveling by railroad at South Fork, motoring on to the site south of Myers Flat. Some of those arriving at South Fork included David Goodewille of Chicago, owner of a box factory and involved in the eastern lumber industry. Charles Quincy of New York, director of the American Forestry Association, and Henry Drinkwater, president of the Pennsylvania Forestry Association, were other prominent attendees. The newspaper observed that the ceremony "was impressive without being at all heavy or monotonous, none of the speakers consuming undue time, and their remarks were carefully listened to by the assemblage with uncovered heads." Speakers included Madison Grant, who observed that "the very air of these groves is redolent with the suggestion of immortality and the trees themselves in their brave resistance to axe and fire symbolize better than anything immortality." Grant urged the American Legion to purchase more groves in honor of fallen soldiers as a better way to honor those men than monuments of stone. Grant stated that it was "the duty for Americans to guard and to preserve what little is left of this [natural] heritage." He ended his comments with an admonition: "[L]et us dedicate ourselves to the task of keeping and preserving in its natural beauty a country which is worth fighting for."[52] A banquet given by the chamber of commerce in Eureka followed the dedication. Speakers at the banquet included Senators Hans Nelson and W.H. Crocker, Assemblyman F.J. Cummings, C. Merriam, Mrs. J.P. Mahan, former California governor George C. Pardee, George Mansfield, Henry Bodkin and Madison Grant. Entertainment was provided by Miss Theoline Pohlson and soprano Miss Muriel Stock.

With the purchase and dedication of the first memorial grove, the Save the Redwoods League found a way to encourage large donations and recognize people who had worked hard for the preservation of the redwoods. Money began to flow into the coffers of the SRL, with members working to find

Named after Deputy State Forester Solon Williams, who helped build the campground, Williams Grove was the first state-owned site allowing camping in Humboldt Redwoods. *HRIA.*

groves to purchase in the targeted areas along the South Fork. The State of California also placed money in the state forestry budget for the express purpose of purchasing threatened redwood groves along the South Fork of the Eel River. Governor William Stephens allocated $300,000 in 1922 for purchase of redwood lands, and the state forestry was able to purchase 2,200 acres of redwood lands desired by the Save the Redwoods League along fourteen miles of the highway for preservation.

These accomplishments were shared by J.D. Grant, who in 1922 published a pamphlet, *Saving California's Redwoods*, for the Save the Redwoods League. J.D. Grant became a board member for the league in 1919; he would serve as president for the organization for twenty-some years. In the pamphlet, Grant reviewed reasons to preserve the redwoods, successes thus far and the need to raise more funds to save more groves. He succinctly stated the reasons to preserve the trees: "[W]e are saving them as trees of indescribable beauty, we are saving them as one of the scientific wonders of the world; finally we are saving them a as a great economic asset of the state and nation."[53] In describing the first memorial grove, Bolling Grove, he wrote:

> *California is trying to do her share to prevent the annihilation of the Redwoods. We have saved a part of the "Highway of the Giants" as part of a state park. We have interested our county governments in the establishment of public parks and memorial groves. We have aroused the consciousness of the nation to the fact that there must be saved a large area— at least 20,000 acres of primitive Redwood forest—to be kept inviolate as a national park. And since we cannot hope to raise more than a fraction of the sum necessary for this purpose through state or county appropriation, the immediate need for Federal action toward the establishment of such a park on behalf of all of our citizens becomes the more manifest.*[54]

The pamphlet also establishes the league's desire to work with the redwood timber industry, as opposed to vilifying the mill owners. The league would maintain a good working relationship with the owners, which helped the league in acquiring land. Equally important, the league established at this point a policy of paying fair market value for the trees. Grant explained, "The work of the Save the Redwoods league has been done in the spirit of fair-play toward the lumbermen and they in turn have given us full cooperation."[55] Grant also noted that lumbermen were "sympathetic toward the object of our movement."[56] He finally added that four lumbermen had already donated land to be preserved.

The official opening of Humboldt Redwoods State Park for visitors came in 1922. The state acquired the land the previous year, and Deputy State Forester Solon Williams was in charge of the new park. Williams was also responsible for purchasing much of the two thousand acres added to the park. The *Ferndale Enterprise* noted that "the work of securing additional tracts is still under way and when all of the tracts have been purchased it is anticipated that the whole section between Dyerville Flats on the north and Miranda on the south will be included in the park reservation."[57] The hope of the SRL members that the redwoods would become a tourist attraction was being realized with the opening of the park. Beyond purchasing the land, Williams along with G.E. Thompson, the first park ranger for Humboldt Redwoods, had seen to the removal of fallen debris and built a headquarters for the park at the Dunn and Dimmick section of the park, just north of Myers Flat, now known as Williams Grove. In addition to housing Thompson, a campfire center and campground were established. Campground spaces "sufficient to accommodate hundreds of machines [automobiles] at one time [were] provided. Fifty tables and fifty large cooking stoves [were] installed as well as sanitary plumbing, electric lights and rest rooms."[58] The editor of the *Ferndale Enterprise* was impressed by the "bandstand and speaker's platform which are being erected on the rim of a natural amphitheatre."[59] Prophetically, the editor noted with the park's opening to the public and construction of the campground that "this great Redwood Park will become the favorite mecca for people from all sections of the United States, as they journey over the only 'Redwood Highway' in the world."[60] Today, more than 100,000 visitors annually from all over the United States, and indeed the world, stop at the visitor center located four miles from Williams Grove. Thousands more come to enjoy the trees.

The following year, more parklands were added, including a grove south of Garberville that was to become known as Richardson Grove State Park. The Save the Redwoods League redoubled its efforts as it met with success. In January 1924, the annual report of the SRL heralded successes thus far in preserving the trees and announced a plan in support of reforestation of cut-over lands. This policy was in line with the timbermen who were replanting their previously logged territories. The Pacific Lumber Company at Scotia, for example, had a large redwood nursery. This goal continues in the current era, as the SRL has sponsored nurseries at Humboldt Redwoods State Park to grow seedlings from locally sourced trees to plant in logged-over areas or cleared for farming, including land near Pepperwood. The SRL also praised the memorial grove program, noting that it helped to both increase the lands preserved and draw attention to the plight of the redwoods. In 1922, Gould Grove was added to Humboldt Redwoods and Bolling Grove was enlarged by donations. State Forester M.B. Pratt claimed in 1923 that "Humboldt Redwoods is becoming one of the most famous parks in the state and will soon rival Yosemite National Park." Pratt also "declared that thousands of tourists are visiting the state owned park in Humboldt…this summer."[61] Members of the Federated Women's Clubs met in Humboldt County that year, traveling to the redwoods along the South Fork as part of the program. As a result, the women pledged to preserve a grove of trees. Similarly, the American Legion held its state convention in Eureka and also went on a tour of the redwoods. Legion members voted to support a redwood national park, agreeing to have each club vote on the matter. Each event helped bring more individuals to the cause of saving the redwoods. Summer also revealed that although the trees preserved in the parks were saved from the axe, they were still vulnerable to natural events, including forest fires. Fire prevention would become one of the duties of the rangers who patrolled the new park. That fall, the league was able to purchase seven acres of redwoods near Phillipsville. This formed the nucleus of F.K. Lane Grove, dedicated the following year.

Franklin K. Lane Grove is dedicated to the former secretary of the interior, who was instrumental in the formation of the National Park Service. *CPHLSC.*

California resident F.K. Lane was appointed secretary of the interior by President Woodrow Wilson. Instrumental in getting Congress to approve the formation of the National Park Service in 1916, Lane also worked closely with members of the Save the Redwoods League. Three years after his death in 1921, his memory was honored with the dedication of the grove. His daughter unveiled a plaque, and officials of the SRL presided over the ceremony. By this time, the grove comprised 195 acres, purchased with a "special fund raised by his friends." He was honored with the "establishment of this grove not only because of his great service to the nation and to the state of California, but also because he was the first president of the Save the Redwoods League and lent his powerful influence to this cause at the time when this movement was beginning." After the grove's dedication, it was opened to the public with several campsites. The goal, according to the *Daily Gazette*, was for Franklin K. Lane Grove becoming a "model camping place which would serve as the standard for similar establishments along the redwood highway."[62]

The Save the Redwoods League's policy of fair treatment to the lumbermen and paying fair market value for the redwoods was severely tested in 1924. The year started on a positive note, with The Pacific Lumber Company donating redwood lands north of the Dyerville Flats to form a 289-acre memorial grove to be dedicated to Simon Murphy, who became controlling owner of the company in 1905. While a beautiful grove, it was not the grove long desired by the league for preservation. The league began negotiations to purchase the large flat that the founders of the league had desired to preserve since 1917. The Humboldt County Board of Supervisors had agreed to help pay for the grove when the manager of TPLCo, Donald McDonald, refused to sell the land to the county in April of that year. McDonald stated that "the company requires every available stick of timber in its ownings to enable it to carry out the lumber program laid out in advance during the next few years, and to part with the Dyerville flat acreage will mean a serious rift in the program."[63] McDonald informed the board of supervisors that "the company would set no price upon the flat as it did not care to sell it at any price."[64] In response, the county filed a "condemnation suit to purchase the Dyerville Flats, an imposing redwood grove on the route of the Redwood Highway." TPLCo in response "obtained an injunction from the United States Court restraining the supervisors from proceeding."[65]

With matters coming to a head in the courtroom, Laura Mahan and her husband worked to help the SRL and the county to acquire the property. In fact, Laura, along with other members of the Women's Save the Redwoods

The mill pond and Mill A of The Pacific Lumber Company (TPLCo), in Scotia, California; TPLCo. owned much of the redwood lands desired by the SRL for preservation. *CPHLSC.*

The plaque memorializing Laura Mahan's and her husband's efforts to preserve Dyerville Flats is near stumps of the two trees cut before they halted logging operations. *Image by author.*

League of Humboldt, stood between the loggers and the trees, giving her husband, James, time to file an injunction in the Humboldt Superior Court to stop the logging. The Mahans learned that timber fallers were in the area of Dyerville Flats, and Laura rushed to the site to find the workers starting to fall timber. She and her fellow members of the Women's SRL of Humboldt stood by the trees while her husband sought to stop the logging in the courtroom. The Mahans and the SRL were able to save the redwoods on the Dyerville Flats because of widespread support of their efforts throughout the county and in the courtroom. In December 1924, the litigants gathered in the offices of Humboldt County district attorney A.W. Hill. An agreement was reached, with the *Ukiah Republican Press* announcing:

> *Dyerville Flat will not be cut—Groves go to the people. Indignation aroused everywhere, when it became known the Pacific Lumber Company of Humboldt County was going to cut the fine grove of giant redwood trees on Dyerville Flat, coupled with strong and prompt action on the part of the district attorney of Humboldt county saved the magnificent tract.*

Giving impetus to the SRL efforts, and causing the lumber company to change its stance, was "the overwhelming sentiment of civic, professional, and social clubs in favor of retaining the Dyerville Flats as a public park and playground for the people forever."[66] The change reflected the growing political impact of women voters and activism of women through clubs, such as the General Federation of Women's Clubs. When formed in 1900, federation founder Mrs. Robert J. Burdette suggested that "federated clubwomen assume as one of the goals the saving of the giant redwoods."[67] Efforts of club women demonstrated their belief and support of that goal. SRL leaders were quick to note the impact women had on their cause and, in 1923, acknowledged that support in their annual report. The chronicle stated that "too much commendation cannot be given the women of Humboldt County for their heroic and untiring efforts to preserve for posterity the redwoods."[68]

The General Federation of Women's Clubs made it its mission in 1925 to raise funds necessary to purchase one more section of the Dyerville Flats, an area lying to the south of the larger stand. Individual club members donated money ranging from $1 to $500, depending on their ability. The clubs were able to raise the $40,000 needed to purchase the grove in a matter of months. Indeed, the money raised was given to State Forester Pratt at the state convention held at Santa Cruz that year. Mrs. John D.

Sherman, president of the California Federation of Women's Clubs, stated, "The General Federation of Women's Clubs played a part last month in winning a decisive victory in Humboldt County, which results in saving one of the finest virgin stands of redwoods intact for all time." In May of that year, Laura Mahan read a telegram to the Humboldt County Board of Supervisors from Mrs. Sherman that "made it plain that the three million club women in the federation are standing back of the Save the Redwood League." Club members were buying a tree in the grove to help purchase more groves. Supporters of the club members included movie stars Mary Pickford and Douglas Fairbanks, each of whom gave $100 for a tree.[69] The money helped with preservation of the Dyerville Flats. In 1929, the club women donated $54,000 to purchase what is now known as California Federation of Women's Clubs Grove. Some of the money raised was also used to hire California architect Julia Morgan, of Hearst Castle fame, to design a large, four-sided outdoor fireplace to be placed in the grove, to be "a symbol of the home center."[70] Construction on the fireplace began in October 1932. The design called for "a mammoth stone chimney with four broad deep fireplaces built under a roof of redwood bark supported by redwood columns." The stone came from a quarry near Garberville.[71]

The dedication of the fireplaces occurred in May 1933, when members of the California Federation of Women's Clubs traveled to the grove. The *Anaheim Bulletin* noted that "the hearthstone is situated off the highway

The four-sided fireplace designed by Julia Morgan at Women's Federation Grove has survived ninety years along the Eel River near Weott, California. *HRIA.*

among the tallest trees and this spot has been allocated to the picnicking party and motorist, although no camping is permitted." Additionally, the paper observed, "a bronze box containing copies of the names of the contributors, several newspaper articles, copy of the Federation News and other valuable papers was sealed in a concrete box at the foot of the hearthstone."[72] Myra Nye for the *Los Angeles Times* described the scene: "Shafts of light from the last gleams of a gray day came from high above the magnificent columns of the redwood trees around the hearthstones. A village choir, singing a capella, added the music of old hymns."[73] The club women also recognized the efforts of Mrs. William A. Fitzgerald in organizing the effort to purchase the grove. Present at the ceremony was Newton B. Drury, who thanked the club members for their ongoing support of preserving the redwoods.

With the Dyerville Flats' preservation seemingly ensured, attention turned, and the battles continued between the various parties over the Bull Creek Flats stands. In February 1925 an agreement was reached whereby the SRL and Humboldt County were able to purchase TPLCo lands involved for $750,000. According to the *San Francisco Examiner*, "Debate at times grew heated, and at one time approached the fighting stage when a question of veracity was raised."[74] Negotiations continued, with the SRL maintaining that it wanted to ensure that the land "owners [would] receive a fair price for their timber and the plan of preservation will involve the minimum inconvenience to the company in its logging operations."[75] To that end, SRL hired forestry expert Major David T. Mason to create a plan to help best preserve the trees.

Despite the acrimony over acquisition of the Dyerville Flats, members of the SRL were happy with the outcome, which led to more groves being purchased. Individuals and organizations became involved in adding to Humboldt Redwoods through the memorial groves, and the state continued to make funds available for purchasing lands. In 1927, the *Napa Journal* observed that "the dedication of groves of trees, rather than monuments to heroes and friends living and dead has increased since the World War."[76] Nearly one thousand acres were added to Humboldt Redwoods between 1922 and 1927. The *Journal* noted that "the Redwood Highway has opened the region to motorists, who have spread the story of the League's effort throughout the nation." Another grove was dedicated to U.S. Senator Felton, across the river from Bolling Grove. Felton's Grove allows a viewshed of old-growth redwoods from Bolling Grove. For the dedication in 1926, a temporary bridge was built. The grove was described "by forestry officials as one of the finest redwood groves in the state." The *Los Angeles Times* observed that "the tract…contains approximately 100 acres and over 1,000,000 feet of redwood timber. It occupies a point of land situated in a picturesque bend of the Eel River, an ideal site for a memorial park."[77] The paper hailed Felton as a California pioneer, coming to the state at the age of seventeen during the gold rush, who had been head of the state mint in San Francisco, was a president of the Southern Pacific Railroad and served two terms in the U.S. Senate. Felton's daughter donated the money to purchase the grove. The grove remains untouched and rarely visited, due to its location.

The year 1927 was a milestone in conservation in California. That year, California State Parks was created as its own department within the state government. Prior to that, state lands were administrated in a haphazard manner, with the redwood parks under the auspices of the state foresters. The Breed State Park Bill, introduced by State Senator Arthur H. Breed, was designed to develop "a comprehensive state park program for California. It means that the state will at once take steps to effect an efficient administration of its disorganized park properties by placing them under one commission empowered to preserve, protect and administer them."[78] The parks were organized under a director, with district superintendents. In 1928, the bill was supplemented by California voters, who agreed to a $6 million bond issue to support the new department, which became known as the California Division of Beaches and Parks. The money was also to be used for the purchase of lands to be protected in the new division.

At Humboldt Redwoods, little changed with creation of the new administration. Park headquarters remained at what is now Williams Grove. In 1929, the grove was officially named for Solon Williams, the state forester who had worked to acquire much of the property along the highway, by State Park Chief Colonel Charles B. Wing. Principal speaker at the dedication was State Forester M.B. Pratt.[79] Williams Grove had two residences, an electric plant and a compound for the state vehicles, in addition to the campground. In 1929, one of the foci for the newly formed agency was addition of lands to Humboldt Redwoods. The headquarters area continued to house park staff. Though now located near Burlington Campground, the park headquarters area continues to provide housing as well as offices for the park's operations.

In 1927, a unique event was presented to promote the need to preserve the redwoods. A pageant, *The Romance of the Redwoods*, written by Garnet Holme and Dan Totheroh, was performed both at Eureka's Sequoia Park and at the Dyerville Flat campfire center. The play "embodies a woodland story whose underlying motive is the preservation of the giant trees and other

Humboldt Redwoods State Park Headquarters is depicted in 1927 at Williams Grove. Due to floods in the twentieth century, none of these facilities remains. *HRIA.*

beauties of nature." Supported by both the SRL and the Eureka Chamber of Commerce, the production featured "[g]irls and women of Eureka… [who] participated in the processionals and dances of the pageant."[80] An upswing in advertising of trips to the redwoods helped to create interest in preservation of the trees and increased visitors to the park in 1927. In April of that year, a group of reporters from the *San Francisco Examiner* traveled to the redwoods, and the trip garnered a full-page spread of redwood images and the tale of their exploits in a "Page Six Sedan." The reporters were very impressed with the redwoods, even in the rain that fell during their trip. John Tiedeman wrote, "The dripping water failed to dampen our enthusiasm for the beauty of the 'redwoods in the rain.'" He observed that the redwoods cared "not a whit for the puny ravings of the storm that failed to sway, much less bend them."[81]

The following year, a very prominent visitor came to take in the beauty of the redwoods. As a presidential election year, 1928 saw Republican candidate and soon-to-be-president Herbert Hoover visit the park. The *San Francisco Examiner* waxed poetic: "Far away from traveled roads with towering redwood trees as a canopy, Herbert Hoover, Republican Presidential nominee slept outdoors tonight at Bull Creek Flat with a party of forty-five of his associates, his secretary, friends and newspapermen." The party was

Founder's Grove became a popular stop for visitors following the dedication. Many came to see Founder's Tree, touted as being the tallest tree in the 1930s. *CPHLSC.*

met at the county line by a motorcycle escort who guided the travelers to the campground. The dinner was cooked for the party by Edwin Freeman, operator of Richardson Grove campground, restaurant and store. The party then slept on cots under the redwoods. The *Examiner* reported that Hoover "thoroughly enjoyed his night in the tall timbers." Upon first arriving at the campsite along Bull Creek, "Hoover pulled out his pipe, stuffed it with tobacco and lit it and then strolled through these ancient creatures of nature. Some of the trees in this virgin forest are more than 2,500 years old, more than 300 feet high and still growing."[82]

The optimism of the 1920s fell in the face of the collapse of the stock market in 1929. The Great Depression brought about many changes for the park, as it did for most of the country. Perhaps the single most impactful event for the park was the purchase of TPLCo lands by the SRL, made possible by a donation of $2 million by John D. Rockefeller in 1931 prior to Franklin Roosevelt's election. The donation—ironically enough, given the acrimony over the purchase of the Dyerville Flats—allowed TPLCo to survive the Great Depression, making it one of only three mills in Humboldt to do so. Rockefeller had been a supporter of the SRL since the early 1920s, when he had visited the forest along Bull Creek, even having lunch with members of the SRL there. He

Image of the Hoover party that camped at Bull Creek Flats. The dinner was prepared by Edwin Freeman from Richardson Grove. *HRIA.*

told a reporter, "I am speechless with admiration. I wasn't prepared for anything so beautiful as the forest we came through today."[83]

Rockefeller was so impressed with the redwoods that he offered to match $1 million raised by the Save the Redwoods League, along with the State Parks Commission, through the efforts of many organizations, including the General Federation of Women's Clubs, the Garden Clubs of America and the Native Daughters of the Golden West. Many of these club women donated small amounts, but the whole added up to match Rockefeller's generous donation. He then donated another $1 million to ensure purchase of the grove. The *Sacramento Bee* observed, "Aside from the matchless beauty and scientific interest of this new Redwood Park, which will make it a goal for tourists and vacationers it is a region of great recreational value."[84] Several papers pointed out that then president Hoover had camped under these redwoods while running for election. The money donated by Rockefeller and others purchased ten thousand acres of forestland, some four square miles. Today, this preserved forestland is the largest stand of old-growth redwood left in the world. This single donation at the time raised the amount of acreage of preserved redwoods in the park to sixteen thousand acres. Recently, the state park system designated much of the forest as State

Wilderness areas. Lands lying north of the Bull Creek Road have been named the Carl A. Anderson Redwoods Natural Preserve after a long-term park superintendent of the region. To the south of the road is the Bull Creek State Wilderness. This designation allows for stricter land management guidelines. The 2010 law states:

> [A]*nd these shall be administered for the use and enjoyment of the people in such manner as will leave them unimpaired for future use and enjoyment as wilderness, provide for the protection of such areas, preserve their wilderness character, and provide for the gathering and dissemination of information regarding their use and enjoyment as wilderness.*[85]

The dedication of Rockefeller Forest was a large affair, attracting more than three hundred people to the trees along Bull Creek. The event actually was held in two places, the first ceremony for dedication of what is now known as Rockefeller Forest and the other to dedicate the tallest tree found at the time to the founders of the Save the Redwoods League. The first

The Rockefeller family enjoying a picnic at Bull Creek Flats in the 1920s. Newton Drury is sitting fourth from left. *Rockefeller Archive Center.*

dedication had many guest speakers, among them John C. Merriam, president of the league. Other speakers included William Colby, chairman of the State Park Commission, and Joseph Grant. Officials from all the organizations who had raised money for the grove were also present. In the afternoon, the group moved to the large flat of trees across the South Fork of Eel River from Bull Creek, to what was then referred to as the Dyerville Flats. There, the tallest tree in that grove was dedicated to the founders of the Save the Redwoods League. The tree had been measured by "Enoch P. French of Eureka, veteran Humboldt County timber cruiser, during the course of an extensive survey undertaken by him on behalf of the Save the Redwoods League to establish the coast redwood as the world's tallest tree. This particular specimen was found to exceed by several feet a number of other redwoods of outstanding height."[86]

CIVILIAN CONSERVATION CORPS WORK IN THE HUMBOLDT REDWOODS

Other changes to the park came about following the presidential election of 1932. With his election, President Franklin D. Roosevelt set forth a series of plans aimed at helping the nation recover from the grips of the economic depression causing high unemployment and company failures. One of the New Deal policies enacted by President Roosevelt benefited the California State Parks in general and the redwood state parks in particular. President Roosevelt's creation of the Civilian Conservation Corps (CCC) helped to create much of the infrastructure in California State Parks, including those in Humboldt County. Franklin explained to Congress:

I propose to create a civilian conservation corps to be used in simple work, not interfering with normal employment, and confining itself to forestry, the prevention of soil erosion, flood control and similar projects. I call your attention to the fact that this type of work is of definite, practical value, not only through the prevention of great present financial loss, but also as a means of creating future national wealth.[87]

To meet the president's initiative, CCC camps were built throughout the United States, where young men were assigned to work on various projects. In April 1933, 166 camps were proposed in California, with one of those camps

A CCC camp was established at Dyerville in 1933. Many of the young men had never seen trees like the redwoods. *HRIA.*

being proposed for Humboldt Redwoods. A tent camp was built at Dyerville, on a field near the river, and the CCC began working on improvements in the area. The large camp accommodated some 350 men. Each park had its own projects; in Humboldt Redwoods, these included building camp stoves at the campgrounds at Williams Grove and Stephens Grove near Miranda, hiking trails, retaining walls and roads. Crews also built a fire lookout on Grasshopper Peak so the groves along Bull Creek could be more readily watched for fire and protected. In 1935, the corps had several large projects. At Burlington, the men were tasked with tearing down the old store and bunkhouse from the time when it was a tie-camp. At Dyerville, they were working on building two bathhouses, living quarters and a laundry. Finally, at Williams Grove, the men were employed building a shower and restroom building.[88] With the CCC camp close to the campground and campfire center at Dyerville, many joined in the evening activities, playing guitars and singing with the tourists. The CCC hired young unmarried men, paying them one dollar per day for their efforts. The men's work was guided by the park rangers.

The rangers continued to work out of their Williams Grove headquarters, where they were able to support one another during the Depression. The pay was held up during the collapse of the economy, according to Florence Traylor Winje, daughter of Carry Traylor, one of the early state park rangers posted at Humboldt Redwoods. He wore badge no. 7. Ms. Winje described her father's job:

> *Those first years my father's duties consisted of some highway maintenance all along Highway 101 from the Mendocino county line to Dyerville Flats, picking up papers along the way. He also shared the duties with the other two rangers as fire department and fish and game authority.…My father maintained the light plant, garage and equipment and patrolled part of Highway 101 as his duties.*[89]

With arrival of the CCC camp, Carry Traylor worked with a CCC crew. Ms. Winje noted that her father "ran a crew of about 25 men daily, year round, who helped clean, pick up and build tables, restrooms and sinks." The other rangers stationed at Williams Grove were Supervisor Glen Thompson and Ranger Mac McLaughlin. They were later joined by Jack Fleckenstein. When at the camp, the men also worked to improve their education. The *Humboldt Times* reported in 1939 of the seventy-eight men stationed at Camp Humboldt Redwood, at Burlington, that nearly half returned home with high school or eighth-grade diplomas or vocational proficiency certificates as a result of the camp's educational program.[90]

Each CCC camp had its own newspaper, filled with notes about the events in and around the camps. Company 925 was originally stationed at Hawkins Bar but moved to Dyerville; here is editor Arthur Montana's take on the move, in an article titled "Brief History of Company 925," in the *Stephens Grove Flash for CCC Camp S.P. 32*. He depicted the company as a child, moving from camp to camp:

> *He had to leave his nice old home at Hawkins Bar and move to a place called Dyerville. So, being an obedient child, and even though it was raining cats and dogs, he just made the move, and finally settled down in a camp called Burlington-Humboldt.*
>
> *So now he had to start in fixing up his new home real nice, as he figured he was going to live here a while. Anyway, he had a good time at this camp, for by this time it was summer again, and there was swimming in the Eel River, hikes to Ghost City, trips to Eureka and Redcrest and Miranda, and girls to see over in the campgrounds and so the time passed nicely and comfortably for awhile.…*
>
> *Once more he recognized his master's voice in a new order to move. Not so bad this time however, as it was only four miles away to a place called*

One fire suppression project of the CCC was the construction of a fire lookout on Grasshopper Peak, above Rockefeller Forest. *CSPA.*

Stephens Grove.... There was a nice schoolhouse to go to, and he could sit around the fire, and he never had to work, that is, on rainy days.[91]

Stephens Grove camp was located where the headquarters for Humboldt Redwoods State Park at Burlington are found today. This group built rock retaining walls near where residences for park staff are located, and these can still be seen. In 1935, Company 925 was divided up and the men sent to different camps; the camp was renamed Burlington-Humboldt. More men were moved there following a flood in 1937 that destroyed the camp at Dyerville.

The crews were very busy while stationed at Dyerville and Stephens Grove. A summary of their work over a two-year period includes:

- 1 footbridge built, Richardson Grove.
- 2 vehicle bridges built—Canoe Creek and Waldon property.
- 10 rods of fences built.
- 8 miles of power line clearing. To bring power into Weott.
- 1 cesspool dug at Dyerville Headquarters.
- 123-foot sewer line.
- 8 camp stoves built for camp use.
- 31 signs placed on highway. To mark boundaries of various groves.

- 2 camp centers built in park camp grounds.
- 3.5 miles of truck trail built on Peavine Ridge.
- 10.2 miles of foot trails built in park area.
- 1,627 square yards of channel clearing in Bull Creek Channel.
- 100 pounds of [redwood] seeds collected for the experimental station at Berkeley.
- 1,612 man days were spent fighting fires (our fire suppression crew at Dyerville deserves special mention).
- 5.4 miles of firebreaks were built in the park area.
- 4.1 miles of fire hazard reduction trailside.
- 209 acres of fire hazard cleared.
- 3 acres of landscaping, planting shrubs etc.
- .3 miles of road obliteration. Old roads in campgrounds blocked off.
- 13 acres of poisonous weeds etc. were eradicated.
- 344 man days were spent in preparing materials for other camps.
- 7.5 miles of park boundary lines were run.
- .2 miles of park roads were drained, etc.
- 410 squard yards of revetment work was done along the south fork of the Eel river to protect the banks.[92]

The CCC crewmen were also critical to firefighting, as they formed a trained crew able to respond quickly with necessary tools. Like the state park system, the California Department of Forestry was in its nascent stage, without manned stations throughout the region. In 1935, the *Burlington-Humboldt Flash S.P. 2* noted that "during the past two months, a total of 35 fires have been suppressed by the 925th suppression crew." The men helped not only with fires in the parks but also those in the surrounding community. The *Flash* observed that "the most damaging of the…blazes was that of Wirta's, which entailed a damage of 64,000 ties and 19,096 cords of wood."[93]

In the May 10, 1935 *Burlington-Humboldt Camp Flash*, the state park project superintendent, Frank Heath, explained the boundaries of the park and what work the men stationed at Burlington would be required to do. His description gives us a snapshot of Humboldt Redwoods in the mid-1930s:

> *The State Park Area extends, roughly speaking, from just north of camp to Richardson Grove, 38 miles south. Also to the west on the Bull Creek Road. One and a half miles west from the Dyerville Bridge is located*

Bull Creek Flat. Another half mile is the Upper Bull Creek Flat where camping facilities are provided to the public—stoves, tables, seats, piped water, and toilets. Another two miles west are located the "Big Tree" and the "Flatiron" tree.

Just across the bridge from camp is the North Dyerville Flat, also a public campground. About 850 feet east on the South Fork road is the "Founder's Tree," said to be the tallest known tree, 364 feet in height.

Then on south along the Redwood Highway comes the following groves: Native Daughters of the Golden West, Perott, Sage, Gould, Fleischman, Mather, Garden Club of America, a tract of 2,552 acres.

Your work will be, to some extent, in and around these groves. Foot trails, foot bridges, vehicle bridges, channel control, reduction of fire hazard and firefighting are the major projects.[94]

The campgrounds mentioned by Heath were all under the old-growth redwoods, but with floods and damage done to the tree roots, these campgrounds were replaced and either located under second-growth or under a mixed forest. Not mentioned by Heath was the work done to bring electricity to Weott from the mill at Scotia or the construction of the Peavine road, where a new tool had been brought from Prairie Creek to help build the road. Another project was building the campfire center at Richardson Grove. The CCC camps were disbanded in 1940, but the trails and retaining walls the men built remain.

Jack Fleckenstein, according to Winje, was in charge of the campground in the Dyerville Flats. The site was close to the main Eel and featured a popular swimming hole. The campground had a large campfire center, and Fleckenstein encouraged "campers to join in the nightly entertainment. He drew much of his talent from the local CCC camp, just across the river."[95] Some of the talent included a young African American man "in his late teens who could tap dance like I have never seen before, except in the movies. He called himself 'Mr. Crabtree.'"[96] Another was a singer Winje felt was as good as Lanny Ross, a popular singer and radio personality during the 1930s and 1940s. The campfire programs were very popular, and soon the rangers had their own programs, attracting visitors who went "from park to park in the evenings to join in the entertainment."[97] Ranger Traylor's campfire program site was north of Myers Flat and was often visited by locals from Scotia and Eureka on the weekends. Winje noted that "this park's big entertainment was its horseshoe tournaments. I would go there with Pop as he cleaned up after the campers left. He had a saying…'People on vacation are the

Opposite: During the 1930s, rangers at Dyerville Campground called on the talents found among the CCC crews. *HRIA.*

Above: The new CCC camp at Burlington, following the destruction of the Dyerville camp in 1937. The CCC helped build many park facilities. *HRIA.*

nicest people in the world because they are so relaxed.'" Winje also wrote that the visitors often "came back year after year and became good family friends through all the years."[98] Perhaps as an impact from the solitude of the redwoods, this tradition continues in the parks.

Winje also observed that the rangers felt themselves to be the guardians of the trees, a feeling still found among the rangers for the redwood state parks. She mentioned that Eleanor Roosevelt came to see the redwood forests, most likely to report back to her husband about the work of the CCC camps. Mrs. Roosevelt toured the region in 1934 on her way from San Francisco to Portland. Winje shared that the fervor to preserve the redwoods had not dimmed during the Great Depression. She noted that people were "buying a tree, an acre, or a grove and naming it after a loved one or an organization. These parks or memorials would be presented to the public for their pleasure with a stone monument." These dedications would be a busy time for the rangers, but they were always an opportunity for speeches. One person she heard frequently was Newton P. Drury, who had become prominent in the Save the Redwoods League. Another common feature was the singing of Joyce Kilmer's "Trees"; in fact, Winje "attended so many ceremonies [she] began to think of 'Trees' as the national anthem."[99]

One dedication Winje would have attended was for the Garden Club of America Grove in 1934. The Garden Clubs of America raised funds helping with the purchase of groves along Bull Creek, but in 1931, it specifically donated money to purchase the groves along Canoe Creek, which flowed into the South Fork of the Eel River between Weott and Myers Flat. The lands were being sold by lumber companies, which were struggling with the Great Depression. The Garden Clubs raised funds for the grove through small donations from members, not unlike the one-dollar donations of the General Federation of Women's Clubs. The effort was at a national level, and the clubs were able to raise enough money to purchase 2,552 acres of redwoods. This initial purchase was added to over the next decades, and the grove now stands at 5,100 acres along the east slopes of Grasshopper Peak. This campaign was the first nationwide effort on behalf of the Garden Clubs of America. Also acquired at this time was the Daughters of the Golden West Grove, acquired as well through the efforts of club women dedicated to the preservation of the redwoods and through small donations.

In December 1937, the Eel River flooded, destroying the CCC camp at Dyerville, along with the park headquarters, which had been moved there following the purchase of the Rockefeller Forest. As a result, some facilities were moved to Burlington, a former split products or tie camp. It was named by L.L. Chapman, owner of the tie camp, "a graduate of Stanford, University [he] aspired to make the region affluent. Hence, he chose to name the new town with a combination of the San Francisco peninsula communities Atherton and Burlingame.[100] Burlington remains Humboldt Redwoods park headquarters to this day. The floods of 1955 and 1964 also affected the park significantly. Despite setbacks created by the floods, the main work of redwood preservation continued. By 1938, 20,157 acres of redwood lands, including Richardson Grove, had been preserved.

According to newspaperman Chapin Hall, Humboldt Redwoods "represent the cream of the state's redwood holdings and the finest known stands of the trees." Chapin continued: "To enter a redwood forest is to transport oneself into a world of thousands of years ago."[101] With an improving economy in the late 1930s, more people were able to experience the redwoods for themselves. Humboldt Redwoods boasted campgrounds at Williams Grove, Upper Bull Creek, North Dyerville Flat, Gould (later Burlington) and Stephens Grove. The largest, Williams Grove, had seventy sites.[102] Helping to promote the park was the announcement that the "Founder's Tree" on Dyerville Flats had been named the tallest tree in the world, at 364 feet.[103]

Enoch Percy French began timber cruising with his father when he was nine years old and worked as timber cruiser for the SRL. *CSPA.*

In order to determine a fair market value for redwood groves purchased by the State Parks and SRL, it was necessary to have a timber cruiser that was respected by the lumbermen, the SRL and state parks. The person who filled the requirements was Enoch Percy French, who served as a ranger and superintendent for Humboldt Redwoods from 1922 to 1953. French was interviewed in 1963 about being a timber cruiser. He explained that "the cruising of Sequoia Semperviron presented unique problems; its large diameter, its near-taperless trunk, and—more important—absented owners living on the opposite side of the continent."[104] French was raised in the redwood country, learning how to be a timber cruiser from his father.

French started timber cruising in 1890, when he was nine years old. He started working in the woods even earlier, when he was eight; his job was to feed the oxen before they hauled logs. In 1906, French started timber cruising by himself. He cruised what is now Rockefeller Forest for The Pacific Lumber Company.

As a cruiser, French had to determine

> *how much commercial timber was there, the mill cuttings, what it would produce for them to sell. In other words if you have ten million board feet on four acres, you might be able to get only five or six million off of it to sell. They want to know that before they put their money down to buy it....The first thing I compute is the number of acres in the entire holding....Then the total number of trees on that particular 40 acres. Next comes how much to discount for breakage and so forth, so that...is the figure for the amount of board feet they will actually be able to take out in net mill out.*[105]

French cruised Bull Creek's watershed, noting in the interview that "section 30...has 200,000 board feet an acre. That's 32 million on 160 acres." He added that "the average forest has from 30 to 40 thousand board feet per acre, and the redwood belt has about 60 thousand, or 65 thousand, maybe on average...you see why it seems somewhat incredible to have

200,000 on one acre. That's a lot of trees."[106] These trees are now protected in Rockefeller Forest.

French was called in to work for the Save the Redwoods League and the State Parks in the early 1920s, when the SRL was working on purchasing its initial groves. Later, when what is now Rockefeller Forest was being considered for fair market value for purchase by the league, John Merriam was concerned when TPLCo said that a cruise had to be increased by 40 percent. Merriam, "who was a scientist and accustomed to precision in measurements, said, 'Any cruise that has to be increased by 40 per cent is not a cruise.'"[107] The increase would be an advantage to The Pacific Lumber Company and cost the SRL more. Thus, French was hired to redo the cruise, which he did based on the actual number of trees and the value of each tree. French's work was approved by both parties, and he continued to work for state parks, doing timber cruising for most acquisitions until his retirement in 1953. Following the flood of 1955, he returned to the park service to help with erosion control.

When first hired, French worked for Solon Williams, deputy state forester, doing timber cruises for both Richardson Grove and Williams Grove. He also cruised much of the timber owned by the Sage Land and Improvement

The Bee River Mill, located in the Bull Creek community, sawed mostly Douglas fir and employed many members of the region. *Courtesy the author.*

Company. Sage, along with The Pacific Lumber Company, owned much of the land that now makes up Humboldt Redwoods. French continued to timber cruise until he became park superintendent in 1931. He was responsible for parks in Del Norte, Humboldt and Mendocino Counties. French worried that he wasn't qualified for the position, as he didn't have a formal education. Colonel Wing, the state director for the parks, responded, "We don't care about that…we're educating them down here in Stanford, we're putting them out by the dozens, and we haven't got a man to come up here to take your place in the redwoods."[108] In fact, French took the job because he believed in the importance of preserving the tall trees. By the time he retired, the State Parks in all three counties had grown to more than sixty thousand acres. Now, Humboldt Redwoods alone is fifty-one thousand acres. One of French's many accomplishments was creating a museum at the park headquarters at Dyerville. There were "all sorts of exhibits of flowers, shrubs, and trees. I took cuts from some trees in there, two thousand year old cuts."[109] Unfortunately, the buildings and exhibits were damaged during the 1955 flood. Twenty-five years later, a visitor center was opened at Burlington campground with similar exhibits. In front of the building is a log with more than eight hundred rings. One of French's concerns during his tenure as park superintendent was the loss of wildlife and wildflowers. Many of the large animals were poached, and bulbs of rare flowers such as the trillium and the redwood lily were dug up. Fortunately, due to park protection, the wildlife and wildflowers are returning, and both the trillium and the lily can currently be found throughout the park in the spring.

Newton Drury and the Save the Redwoods League continued to acquire redwood property during the next decade; French was the timber cruiser for most of this. The groves around what is known as High Rock were purchased in 1940. With the advent of World War II, land acquisition slowed but did not stop. More land was purchased between Dyerville and Redcrest. As part of the war effort, and as a call for peace as well as to celebrate the holidays, Founder's Tree was highlighted with floodlights following the bombing of Pearl Harbor in 1941, "making it the tallest living Christmas Tree."[110] The following year, the tree lighting was marked with a candlelit ceremony. It was sponsored by the Fortuna Rotary Club and the State Parks Commission. By 1945, the tree lighting had expanded significantly. The tree was lighted with fifty thousand watts of lights on December 11. The twenty-five-member a capella choir from Humboldt State College, under the direction of Charles Faulkner, provided music for the event. The program was broadcast by KSFO of San Francisco and transmitted across the Armed Forces radio as well. In addition to the choir, the program consisted of "a dramatic descriptive and historical narrative about the 364-foot giant and the surrounding area." It was written by Norman Kramer and was narrated by KSFO news editor Austin Fenger.[111] The *Oakland Tribune* waxed poetic about the event: "The total potential audience will number many hundreds of millions of persons. So as you listen to the beautiful Christmas story with its message of a new world of peace and brotherhood you will be aware that it comes to you from a living symbol which has survived and triumphed over all the tragedies and sorrows that have shaken the human race during the long generations of its climb toward light and reason in the affairs of man."[112]

Following the end of World War II, camping and exploring in the great outdoors gained in popularity. Williams Grove became a favorite spot for visitors. It became so popular that a fifteen-day camping limit had to be instituted there during the height of summer. In 1951, the *Stockton Evening and Sunday Record* noted, "The Humboldt Redwoods especially attract many visitors each year and the various groves dotting Highway 101 afford camping grounds all along this route."[113] With success comes consequences, and by 1953, traffic along the Redwood Highway was becoming very congested. According to Newton Drury, "Millions travel the Redwood Highway to see these wonderful forests. It is unthinkable that in providing a highway to these redwoods the redwoods themselves should be destroyed."[114] The Division of Transportation wanted to widen the road through the park. During summer months, locals, logging trucks, lumber trucks and tourists all contrived to slow down the travelers on the road. In 1955, it was proposed to build a four-lane highway from Richardson Grove to Pepperwood in the north, to bypass the "Redwood Highway" and allow ease of transportation for all users of the road.[115] Despite opposition from the Save the Redwoods League and the Garden Clubs of California, the four-lane highway was completed in 1965. Some of the trees removed were used to restore Fort Ross on the Sonoma coast after it had been burned by arsonists.

The year 1955 marked a series of disasters in Humboldt County. During the summer, large fires burned in the region, including into Rockefeller Forest. December saw the largest flood to date along the Eel River. Humboldt Redwoods was the hardest hit of the redwood state parks, with many large trees falling due to being undermined by the waters, according to Newton Drury. When the floodwaters receded, it was clear that the damage was caused by erosion stimulated by logging done west of the park. This set in motion many attempts to alleviate the damage and protect the trees in future floods. These attempts included rock gabions, placing stumps in the creek

During World War II, the Founder's Tree was lit with electric lights, and Christmas carols were sung in a call for peace around the world. *CPHLSC.*

Above: Building a four-lane highway allowed more accessibility to the region but also meant that many trees were cut to build it. *HRIA*.

Opposite: Weott residents look over their flooded homes and businesses in December 1955. By this time, most of the land west of the town was in Humboldt Redwoods State Park. *CPHLSC*.

bed and lining Bull Creek with large rock. None was successful, leading the state to make the decision to implement a program of eminent domain to acquire the entire Bull Creek watershed. Other damages to the park occurred at the Stephens Grove and William's Grove campgrounds. The damage was so severe at Williams Grove that the campground did not open during the summer of 1956. Stephens Grove never reopened as a campground. There was other damage to trails and roads close to the river.

To alleviate the loss of campsites, the park system decided to build a new campground, Hidden Springs, located near Myers Flat away from the river

and flood danger. Opened in 1959 with ninety-nine sites, the campground featured shower facilities as well as layouts for the campsites "to provide ideal screening from adjoining sites for desired privacy in the middle of nature's own handicraft."[116] Fifty-five more sites were added after the 1964 flood. The campground was named Hidden Springs because it had been difficult to find an adequate water supply for the campground—the redwood trees would absorb all the water from the springs. Williams Grove was turned into a day-use area, as the damage done to it was too great to repair. It was closed to the public from 1955 to 1959. The day-use area remains popular as an access point to the Children's Forest, a grove of 1,279 acres that was selected in the 1930s as a dedicated grove, as it was felt this would be a place children would enjoy.

In 1960, the four-lane bypass of the now severely congested Redwood Highway was completed to the point that the original highway was renamed "Avenue of the Giants." A dedication ceremony was held on the Eel River bar at High Rock, between Dyerville and Redcrest on the newly named avenue. In attendance was California governor Edmund

At the 1960 dedication of the Avenue of the Giants, Governor Edmund G. Brown was one of the keynote speakers. *CSPA.*

G. Brown and Will Rogers Jr., chairman of the State Park Commission. Brown gave the principal address, noting that redwoods were "one of the state's greatest assets." Brown believed that the new highway would "open up new sources of recreation on land which the state has owned for decades. Trucks can go about their business without violating the quiet of the forests. Travelers will be able to drive from San Francisco to Eureka at Freeway speed limits and with safety. Tourists with their families can enjoy their visits here without damage from highway traffic." Brown was also moved by the redwoods, observing, "On this quiet bar of the Eel River we are close to a magnificent forest, in which some of the world's tallest trees face extinction." Referring to the plans to acquire the Bull Creek Watershed, Brown commented, "If you could compare the site as it is today with photographs taken 10 years ago you would be appalled by the destruction. Already more than 500 huge redwoods and many smaller trees have been lost. This senseless waste must be stopped. California will not permit the forest to disappear, either through floodwaters or strangulation by rock and gravel which choke the roots." Brown hoped to balance the lost income to logging with tourism. Other dignitaries at the ceremony included State Senator Carl Christensen, Assemblyman Frank Belotti and SRL officers Arthur Connick (president) and Newton Drury (secretary).[117]

The flood of 1964 changed the purchasing plans of the SRL. Heralded as a "thousand-year flood," heavy rains fell on already saturated ground, causing the Eel River to rise higher than it had in 1955. The floodwaters swept away homes, businesses and bridges. Between Dyerville and Fernbridge, all bridges were swept away or left unstable. Once the floodwaters receded and road damage began to be repaired, Humboldt Redwoods State Park employees began to survey damage done to the redwood forests, especially along Bull Creek in Rockefeller Forest. Floodwaters caused great devastation for the park and the trees. The *Sacramento Bee* reported that "five feet of new silt lies on Bull Creek in the Rockefeller Forest." Additionally, "two to five feet of gravel covers the entire Bull Creek Basin….Steps are being taken to protect the Rockefeller forest from the millions of tons of gravel being washed downstream."[118] Work done after the 1955 flood had helped stabilize the banks, but still many redwoods fell as the banks of the Eel and all the small creeks feeding into it were ravaged by the high waters.

Again, as after the 1955 flood, the state park rangers and crews worked long hours to remove the sticky silt from the day-use areas and roads near the river. This included removing several feet of material from the four fireplaces at Women's Federation Grove. Trails were reestablished and bridges replaced on routes through the forests. The greatest losses were the hundreds of trees due to flood damage. Many streams feeding into Bull Creek "blew out," leaving behind severely eroded hillsides. With none of the strategies tried to stabilize the watershed proving successful, the efforts by the state to acquire the area increased. Additionally, logging continued in the lands not owned by the state, further contributing to the damage done to the giant trees. In the late 1950s and early 1960s, there were two mills at Bull Creek and a large mill at Myers Flat, in addition to the large mill of Pacific Lumber in Scotia. Other local mills included a large one at

The 1964 floodwaters are captured by this picture; to the left is Women's Federation Grove and Rockefeller Forest, and to the right is Founder's Grove. *Charlie Thomas.*

Redcrest and north of Rio Dell at Metropolitan. Many of the mills sawed Douglas fir, but the erosion caused by logging directly affected the large groves of redwoods along the rivers and streams closer to the Eel. This had been made vastly apparent by the damages done by the 1955 and 1964 flood. Through eminent domain, the land comprising the Bull Creek watershed was purchased with the support of the SRL. After the parks acquired the land, they caused bitter feelings among the locals as they bulldozed and burned the residences, including the local church, as they worked to return the land to a pre–European settlement ecology. Over the past fifty years, the land has slowly recovered, and floods along the Eel are not as devastating to the redwoods. However, to a certain extent, local animosity remains.

Following acquisition of the Bull Creek Watershed, the State Parks began to add visitor facilities. In addition to adding fifty campsites to Hidden Springs, a new traditional campground, Albee Creek, opened in 1966 with thirty-two campsites, at the site of the Gabeler Homestead, where some of the old orchards still grow. Other campgrounds added reflected a new type of visitor, one interested in more remote camping or hiking opportunities. These improvements included campsites; a horse camp at Cuneo Creek, formerly the Lewis family homestead; and

Damage caused by floodwaters in 1964 to the banks of Eel and the trees that grew alongside. *CSPA.*

building trails for the use of riders, designating others to be multi-use. The Environmental Camp sites were a combination of car camping and backpacking. These sites were more remotely located, and although a car could be parked nearby, the campers have to pack things a short distance to their designated site. Humboldt Redwoods has five of these sites. The final type of campground were true backpack sites, where campers hiked into the various campsites. The park has five trail camps, all located within the Bull Creek watershed.

Starting in 1972, Humboldt Redwoods also became the sight of the biannual Avenue of the Giants Marathon, attracting thousands of runners to the region in May and October every year. The first marathon had thirty-two runners and now sees several thousand. The Six Rivers Running Club wanted to have a race that would serve as a qualifier for the 1972 Olympic trials. The race is now a qualifier for the Boston Marathon. The club felt that the course along the Avenue of the Giants from Dyerville to Albee Creek and along the Avenue to Myers Flat would be ideal: "The area was relatively flat, with a few interesting hills; the scenery was unsurpassable; and traffic control would be no problem. Early May would be an ideal time to hold a marathon there. The weather would be warm, but not hot; and hopefully the rainy season would be over."[119] Since the first race, many have run along the avenue, enjoying the redwoods as they cover the course.

Protecting the Redwood Forests

Since its inception in 1927, the position of state park ranger has evolved to meet the challenging demands of protecting the State Parks. In 1972, the state park system determined that law enforcement was necessary to protect the parks and visiting public. Rangers now receive standard peace officer training. Typical duties include "interpreting the natural and historical features in a park, conducting guided tours and campfire programs, developing and maintaining exhibits and publications materials, conducting search and rescue operations, reducing hazards to public safety, implementing training programs…administering park areas, and performing many other activities to help insure a pleasant and safe experience for visitors."[120] With the ranger focus on law enforcement and public protection, other staff were hired to maintain the infrastructure of the park system.

In Humboldt Redwoods, one of the greatest influences on changing the ranger position was the rise of the illegal marijuana industry. In the late 1970s and early 1980s, growers discovered that if they grew on the state park, they would be harder to find and would not lose their property, as that was one of the penalties at the time. These illegal grows were scattered throughout the park, causing damage to the redwoods' fragile ecosystem. Illegal pesticides and fertilizer were dumped into streams, creeks were diverted to provide water to the marijuana gardens and deer and rodents that damaged crops were shot. When streams were diverted for watering gardens, it changed the ecosystem below the diversion.

An unidentified ranger works to eradicate an illegal marijuana grow. These gardens often caused severe damage to the forest's ecosystem. *Jim Baird.*

State Park Ranger II Jim Baird worked at Humboldt Redwoods when the illegal marijuana grows were becoming a problem. He explained:

> *In the 1980s and '90s the state park rangers were tasked with trying to monitor and eradicate illegal marijuana grows occurring in our parks. Marijuana was not legal for medical or personal use in the state during those years. Our main concerns with these grows were resource destruction, water diversion, use of poisons to reduce predators and deer, trash and pollution from camp waste and fertilizers, and public safety. Run-down seasonal campsites often existed in these remote grow sites, and the area around the site was often littered with months of trash accumulation. Water*

tanks, hundreds of yards of plastic pipe, grow pots and animal fencing were found throughout the landscape.

Most of the illegal grows were not in locations where park visitors were likely to come across them if they stuck to the park trails and fire roads. However, if a person were to walk up creeks or hike cross country there was the possibility of ending up in an illegal grow site. We did find weapons and toxins in grow sites. We also found booby traps such as shotguns with trip wires secured to trees along paths to the gardens.

Most of our operations were very labor intensive with small crews. Most of our reconnaissance was done on foot, usually in trail-less areas, hiking up or down small creeks or to areas with known springs. Typically 1–2 rangers would spend much of their time in spring and early summer scouting for illegal grows in the park backcountry. Rarely were these gardens removed until mid or late summer. We didn't have staff on hand to remove them as we found them, and if we removed them early, many growers would just relocate and start over. By doing eradication operations in mid and late summer we contained the problem better, and the growers would likely not relocate that season.

When we were ready to start formal eradication efforts, we would reach out to borrow ranger staff from other parks or districts to help us. In a typical summer at Humboldt Redwoods SP we would have 10–15 grows to eradicate with these teams. Six to ten Rangers would go as a team, locate the garden, watch for people or activity, then go in and remove the plants, campsites, garbage, plastic pipe, fencing and water tanks. At times this meant carrying things out over several miles of steep and brushy terrain. We tried to get motorcycles, quads or 4x4s as close as we could when we were ready to start hauling debris out.

We would make a couple of arrests per season. To successfully make a significant number of arrests would have required many more staff and much more surveillance than we had time or staff to devote to the program. Marijuana growing operations coincide with peak busy seasons for the parks.

We were not a formal partner in any state wide marijuana eradication program such as CAMP. Our focus on marijuana eradication was within the boundaries of the state parks. But on a few occasions we did arrange for use of a helicopter to airlift hundreds of pounds of marijuana plants out of trailless backcountry locations.[121]

Marijuana grows were often filled with trash, plastic pipe and fertilizers that damaged the redwoods. Rangers confiscated a sawed-off shotgun at this grow. *Jim Baird.*

With the legalization of marijuana in California, illegal grows are no longer the concern they once were.

Currently, rangers are working to ensure that other landowners do not encroach on the redwood forest and that trees and burls are not being cut. In the winter, when the river levels are higher, unscrupulous individuals often saw through trees that have fallen into the river and tow them with a boat to a place they can pull the trees from the river. Sometimes called "river pirates," these individuals then saw the logs into lumber and sell it. The rangers are there to protect the forest, and the fallen giants are part of the park's ecosystem.

Ranger duties vary from day to day, and talking to the public about the redwoods remains a constant. Ranger Ron Jones began working at Humboldt Redwoods State Park in 1986. At that time, according to Jones, "Park ranger duties included patrol of the 50,000-acre park, leading nature walks, campfire programs, overseeing seasonal workers, assisting and training volunteers at the visitor center, [patrolling] campgrounds and day use areas."[122] Jones's favorite part of his job was sharing with the public about the redwoods and their unique ecology. He often led nature walks,

Logs fallen into the Eel were often targets of river pirates, who cut the logs, floating them to where they could pull them from the river. *HRIA.*

which could be "anywhere in the park....These talks/walks could be as little as 10 minutes up to 2 hours. I especially enjoyed giving these talks, and several times people would come up to me after the talk/walk and say, 'You really enjoy talking about the redwoods don't you?'" One event that found Jones talking to many travelers about the redwoods came in March 1991. On the morning of March 25 that year, a visitor to the park stopped at park headquarters, telling staff, "The Dyerville Giant had fallen." Jones was "amazed to hear that, so [he] immediately drove over there and sure enough, it had met its demise the night before. It is almost more impressive laying on the ground for a totally different perspective to its tremendous size."[123] After the tree fell, word spread, with travelers coming from all over the world to

Alders and redwoods branch over Bull Creek, revealing that the creek is recovering from damages done by the 1955 and 1964 floods. *Author image.*

take in the sight. Jones and other rangers were on hand to both talk about the trees and protect the fallen giant. Jones observed in the *Times-Standard* that "several people were caught trying to smuggle pieces of the fallen tree out of the park…one man who had a huge chunk of the giant slung over his shoulder. When stopped, the man said he wanted it for his front porch."[124]

The redwoods continue to attract visitors, and one way that the redwoods began to be appreciated was through film. Although film studios had made pictures in the redwoods dating back to 1919's *Valley of the Giants*, based on the book by Peter A. Kyne, it wasn't until the 1950s that movies and advertisements were filmed on a regular basis in the park. Films shot in and around Humboldt Redwoods include 1967's *Gnome Mobile* and 2013's *After Earth*. Many commercials are also shot among the redwoods. However, filming is not always easy. When *Gnome Mobile* was filmed in Rockefeller Forest, California Division of Forestry ranger Harry Pritchard was en route to a fire west of the park. The film crew tried to stop him, as they were filming. Pritchard responded that he was on his way to a fire and told them to move out of his way. They continued to protest, so Pritchard radioed the firetrucks behind him to not slow down and to go on to the fire as code three, meaning with lights and sirens. The film crew learned that fires take precedence and had to re-film that section of the movie.[125]

Humboldt Redwoods continues to grow as SRL finds more land to purchase. It is now the third-largest state park and the largest of the redwood state parks. It remains a destination for many to come and enjoy the redwoods. In 2023, the Facebook page for "Magical Bucket List Destinations" listed Humboldt Redwoods State Park as one of its "Bucket List Destinations."[126] The trails built by the CCC camps are being maintained and allow access into the large groves of redwoods along Bull Creek and elsewhere in the park. The reason for the hard work of the SRL can be seen along the Avenue of the Giants and in Rockefeller Forest. Humboldt Redwoods State Park is now 51,676 acres, with 186 miles of trails. The Humboldt Redwoods State Park Interpretive Association was formed in 1979, and a visitor center for the park opened in 1980. This organization continues to help visitors learn about the redwoods and what makes them unique. While many of the lumber mills that once milled the tall trees have been closed, the trees remain, preserved for posterity in all their magnificence.

Chapter 3

RICHARDSON GROVE STATE PARK

In 1922, the SRL purchased a grove near the border of Mendocino County, now known as Richardson Grove State Park. Named for the twenty-fifth California governor, Friend Richardson, the grove became very popular with tourists and locals alike, as dances, campfire programs and other activities were held in the grove, several miles south of the town of Garberville.

Unlike other redwood state parks, Richardson Grove began as a resort, originally owned by Henry Devoy. Devoy leased his property to Edwin R. Freeman in 1920. Freeman and his wife came to Humboldt County following the 1906 earthquake in San Francisco. He and his wife established a popular photography business in Eureka, and Mrs. Freeman was known for her images of redwoods, many of which were used by the Save the Redwoods League to publicize the plight of the trees. Both became popular photographers, with Edwin helping in 1915 to "form the World's Fair Photographic Department and complete charge of sales…since that time he has specialized in convention photography and was official photographer for the national Democratic convention in San Francisco. He [held] the same position with the California Save the Redwoods League, the Pacific Lumber Company and the Stanford Illustrated Review."[127] The Freemans divorced in 1915 after she was alleged to have been seen kissing former Illinois governor Yates. She continued with photography, while her husband sought other ways to make a living. Thus, Edwin leased land from Devoy, building a store, a dining room and fifteen cabins to serve the needs of the travelers

Harry DeVoy established the resort area now known as Richardson Grove. In 1918, Edwin Freeman leased DeVoy's land, managing the cabins, a store and a restaurant. *CPHLSC.*

on the newly constructed "Redwood Highway." Henry Devoy purchased it from the Reed family, near the Mendocino County line, along the Redwood Highway. Devoy was from Ferndale and had lived in the Fort Seward area, owning property throughout the region.

Freeman was interested in attracting tourists to his new resort and was aided by the highway going past his business. For example, in 1923, the *Fresno Morning Republican* shared details of a trip taken to the redwoods by Mrs. May Case of Clovis and Mr. and Mrs. J.P. Kelly of Modesto. The travelers were impressed by Freeman's lodge, observing, "This is one of nature's choicest beauty spots…there are free campgrounds, free water, free swimming, free entertainment each evening when the campers gather about a huge bon fire and a lecturer provides food for thought."[128] Freeman was often the speaker, informing about the redwoods or other "pertinent topics."[129] Other amusements offered included dancing, provided free of charge. Tourists appreciated the cabins, which were rented, and the "dining room where excellent meals are served." Additionally, food supplies could be purchased at the resort's store.[130]

The Save the Redwoods League purchased 120 acres of redwood land from Devoy in 1922 for $25,000.[131] It was dedicated to Friend Richardson, who served as California governor from 1923 to 1927. A supporter of the

Edwin Freeman advertised the resort through his postcards and photographs. He lectured about the redwoods during the winter in the San Francisco Bay Area. *HRIA.*

Save the Redwoods movement, Freeman lobbied to have the new state park named after Richardson, who was also a supporter. Richardson traveled through the park in 1925 on his way to the Fortuna Rodeo. With the grove lying farther south than the other groves recently added to Humboldt Redwoods in 1923, "State Forester M.B. Pratt announced...that the state board of forestry...authorized the drawing up of a new contract whereby Richardson Grove in Humboldt Redwood Park will be leased to E.R. Freeman of San Jose for a period of ten years."[132] The terms of the lease included a plan to improve visitor facilities and for the state to receive 5 percent of the gross receipts. The paper noted that the dining hall had been recently completed. Additionally, the lease included "a provision making it possible for the state to purchase the buildings at 50 percent of cost price at the end of the ten-year period." In 1922, the resort made $8,000, and Pratt felt that the current contract did "not give Freeman a fair show in payment for the work he is doing in the park."[133] In July 1924, 460 people were camped at Richardson Grove one evening.[134] Freeman continued to operate the park as more of a resort than just a campground until the 1930s.

In 1926, the Save the Redwoods added eighty acres to the park, thanks to a donation by G. Frederick Schwarz of New York City. Schwarz, "a philanthropist deeply interested in the public park movement," also donated a memorial grove in Del Norte County, dedicated to Henry S. Grave. His donation at Richardson Grove added beach access for campers. The *Sacramento Bee* noted that "Richardson Grove has grown to be a favorite camping spot for tourists and vacationers because of the heavy growth of trees. With the addition of the beach, the campers may now emerge directly from a dense forest, cool even on a mid-summer day, to the sandy beach to enjoy swimming in the warm sunshine."[135] With all of its facilities, Richardson Grove became very popular very quickly. It also became a highlight for many publicity and tourism junkets. One such event in 1924 by the San Francisco Auto Club members had the travelers staying at Richardson Grove, entertained there with a "special Indian dance by some Hoopa Indians brought from the Round Valley Reservation."[136]

Native Americans were also in the forefront in 1927 and 1928 when the Redwood Empire Association, a group that promoted tourism along Highway 101 north of San Francisco, sponsored an ultramarathon, a 480-mile race from San Francisco to Grant's Pass, Oregon. Called the Great Indian Marathon, the race was used to promote the region north of San Francisco. The *Napa Valley Register* observed, "This unusually long-distance contest is possible because of the pleasant coolness of the Redwood Highway during the summer months, for the Redwood Highway leads through over 100 miles of giant redwood trees." The paper added, "97 per cent of the world's redwoods stand in the Redwood Empire, and there are many miles of ocean shore line bordering the highway."[137] Typical of the era, the race, although featuring Native Americans and their running abilities, was racist in nature. Competing in the race were Karuk and Zuni Native Americans; however, they were assigned stereotypical names, and no attempt at honoring the actual tribes was made. The route for the race ran through Richardson Grove, what is now the Avenue of the Giants, the Newton Drury Parkway, Del Norte Redwoods and Jedediah Smith Redwood State Parks. Movie cameras of the day captured the contestants as they ran through Richardson Grove. When a tourist watched a runner come through the grove at 2:00 a.m., she reported it back to her home newspaper about the highly publicized and popular event.[138] The winner of the race, given the moniker "Mad Bull," was actually John Southard. He was from Happy Camp on the Klamath River. For his efforts, he was awarded $1,000 upon his arrival in Grant's Pass.[139] The race was not repeated after the second annual event in 1928. However, in 1987, the race was re-created by six alumni of Grant's Pass High as part of the school's centennial celebrations. John Southard was at the finish line to congratulate the runners. The 1987 runners were all in

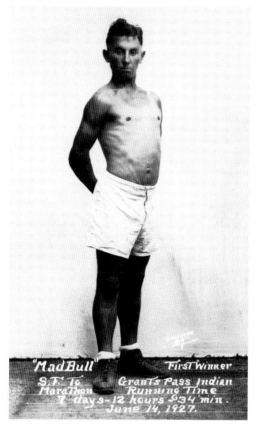

"Mad Bull" First Winner
S.F. To Grants Pass Indian
Marathon Running Time
7 days-12 hours 934 min.
June 14, 1927.

Left: John Southard, called "Mad Bull" for the Great Indian Marathon, won the 1927 480-mile race in seven days, twelve hours and thirty-four minutes. *CPHLSC*.

Below: Campers enjoy camping at Richardson Grove; note how fallen branches are removed, different from today's practice of letting branches decay into the forest floor. *HRIA*.

Camp at Richardson Grove, 327.

agreement, according to one relay participant, Wayne Marrow: "The longer we were out there, the more we realized there was a hero on this course, and it wasn't any of us. There is a hero of this 1987 run, and he is this man right here, John 'Mad Bull.'"[140]

Richardson Grove had been designated as part of Humboldt Redwoods, and with the formation of the state park system in 1927, the ranger staff at Williams Grove began to patrol the park. Freeman continued to operate Richardson Grove as a resort without becoming a park ranger. He was, however, designated as a deputy fire warden and deputy sheriff.[141] In 1927, he applied his firefighting skills helping save guests at the nearby Hartsook Inn. The inn, owned by Fred Hartsook, was destroyed, along with a post office and garage buildings, but the efforts of Freeman and others saved the nearby cottages and prevented the fire from spreading into the redwoods and into Richardson Grove. Those staying at the hotel "left hurriedly in scanty attire and were moved to a camp in Richardson Grove."[142] Undoubtedly, the hotel guests were able to find what they needed, as Richardson Grove that year was described as being "the best equipped up-to-date in every comfort of any of the state parks in the division."[143] In 1928, another fire threatened the grove but was confined to fifty-five acres. Again, Freeman must have been involved in suppressing the fire.

At that time, the road to the grove was mostly gravel, with travelers often staying at one place for several days or even weeks. Thus, the campground became a favorite destination camp. Swimming in the river was a popular activity. The Redwood Empire Association held an annual convention in 1928, with many participants staying at Richardson Grove. The following year, Richardson Grove was the second-most visited of the California State Parks, with 26,460 people visiting the park during the twenty-week summer season, from May to September. The most popular park that year was the Santa Cruz Redwood Park, Big Basin. The rest of the Humboldt Redwoods State Parks saw 1,894 visitors in seventeen weeks, according to the *Redding Searchlight*.[144] The year 1929 also saw Richardson Grove featured at the centennial exhibition of the Massachusetts Horticultural Society in Boston. The display featured a panorama of "a scene in Richardson grove….A redwood stump, some ten feet through is in the exhibit." Another event took place at the grove when Dr. Fletcher Watson, a Methodist reverend, presented a religious service at the campfire center. This event became a regular feature of state parks during the 1940s, with Sunday services presented by different denominations at outdoor campfire centers.

Swimming remains a popular activity at Richardson Grove, as depicted in this Freeman photo from the 1920s. *HRIA.*

As with Humboldt Redwoods, tourism slowed but did not diminish during the Great Depression. Freeman continued to attract customers with his evening entertainments, including his campfire programs. Guest speakers included members of the Save the Redwoods League, including Dr. Merriam and Newton Drury. Drury had become the executive director of the league in 1919, a position he held until 1938. He worked tirelessly to promote the tall trees and the groves that had been saved, drawing attention to the redwoods being harvested.

In 1932, California governor "Sunny Jim" Rolph started labor camps to alleviate some of the stress being placed on state resources by out-of-work men, a precursor to the Civilian Conservation Corps that President Roosevelt unveiled the following year. The *Sacramento Bee* explained:

> *Breadlines of larger cities will furnish the recruits for California's forty-three state labor camps, which will open as soon as the state receives its first soaking rainfall. The men, single and transient mostly from other states will be removed from the streets of the cities where they are a charity problem and placed in the camps to build fire trails and engage in watershed protection activities.... Twenty-three of the camps will be situated in the northern part of the state and twenty in the south and will house 6,250 men who will work in exchange for shelter, food, clothing and tobacco.*

In Humboldt County, four camps were established—at Perrott Creek, north of Dyerville, accommodating 250 men; Bull Creek, 50 men; Richardson Grove, 100 men; and Burlington camp, 100 men.[145] These men began the work that was soon taken over by the Civilian Conservation Corps. The camps were not a huge success, as the men were not paid, and they could leave to look for work on their own volition. The camps lasted for only about four months.

However, shortly after the California labor camps were dismantled, the Civilian Conservation Corps was established by President Roosevelt. As a result, the campgrounds and trails at Richardson Grove benefited from the efforts of the Civilian Conservation Corps camp at Dyerville. Companies 925 and 732 worked at Richardson Grove to build camp stoves, tables and campsite cupboards. The men also worked on rebuilding the store and kitchen.[146] As a result of the CCC's work, designated campsites were created, as opposed to the more open, "camp where you like under the trees" campground that had been operated by Freeman. The CCC also built a restroom and improved the water system for the campground. In 1935, the CCC workers were working on an "open air theater, plans for dance platform, stoves for campers, rail fence near headquarters."[147] By 1937, Richardson Grove had 250 campsites, courtesy of the work of the CCC. These included the camp across the river, the Tan Oak Campground, and Huckleberry, which was located more under the redwoods.

To help promote visitation to the redwood parks in 1933, the Save the Redwoods League published an itinerary for travelers to ensure that they saw the best of the redwood state parks. The guide included identifying when wildflowers would be in bloom, including rhododendrons and ferns found later in summer. The *Sacramento Bee* noted that the "itinerary describes all the redwood groves from Richardson Grove northward to Grant's Pass." An article in the *San Francisco Examiner* also lauded the redwoods and Richardson Grove. Reporter Frank Lyman wrote, "Unforgettably etched in the memory of motorists who travel the Redwood Highway through California are pictures of forests where twilight is perpetual; where ferns seem shoulder high where flowers have made shift to bloom without the sun." Lyman also felt that Richardson Grove was one of the best stops along the highway.[148] Part of the charm of Richardson Grove was the entrance to the restaurant through a "goose-pen," one of the burned-out sections of a living tree.[149]

Keeping tourists returning year after year to Richardson Grove, even during the Depression, were the variety of facilities. The *Yucaipa News-Mirror*

The campfire center at Richardson Grove was built by the CCC in the mid-1930s. The crew traveled from Burlington to work on the facilities. *HRIA.*

The access through the "goose-pen" to the restaurant at Richardson Grove is shown in this Freeman photo. *HRIA.*

reported in 1935, "There are campgrounds with nearly every variety of camping equipment, a swimming pool, a dance floor and overnight cabins. There is a good bathing beach and the fishing in this vicinity is good. The park offers free guide service and trips are made daily over the park trails. Another feature is the campfire circle every night."[150] These thoughts were reiterated the following year when Charles Perrine shared his experiences at the Grove in the *Oakland Tribune*. He pointed out that more modern cars and straightened roads had cut the trip from Oakland to only five hours, an improvement allowing more people to visit the park and enjoy its offerings. Perrine humorously observed:

> [T]*he redwoods will provoke as much thought as you like in indulging in. You can look at them and say, "oh my what big trees," and take a swim in the river and let it go at that. You can wonder how it would be to climb to the top of one, and what you could see from up there. Or you can wonder what this funny old world was doing when these trees were saplings. The more you think about it, the smaller and more insignificant you become. The redwoods are not a good place to nurture an ego.*

Perrine also noted all the activities, including horseback riding and sunbathing; mostly, he urged all, "If you haven't been up there, don't let another summer go by without going—and those who have been there don't need any urging."[151]

However, not everyone who came to see the redwoods "saw them," according Chapin Hall in 1937. In a series he was writing about the State Parks that year, he noted that at Richardson Grove there was debate about widening the road to accommodate those who thought the "'doing' the redwoods meant driving through them at sixty miles an hour." Chapin related a story of an encounter between one such visitor and Division Superintendent Percy French. According to Chapin, French was standing

> *in the heart of Richardson Grove surrounded by 300 foot giants as a New York Car came to a creaking halt. "Where are the big trees we've been hearing about?" demanded the driver who said they had driven in from the north. That meant they had passed through 100 miles or so of the finest specimens. "If you haven't seen 'em guess they must be down south," the superintendent replied. "Okeh, we've got another 200 before dark." And the visitors, who had crossed a continent without seeing a thing but the road ahead, were off in a cloud of dust.*[152]

Chapin felt it was sacrilege to cut the trees just to widen the road to accommodate such visitors. Ironically, this debate continues to the present day, as a proposed bypass has yet to be built, and all traffic on Highway 101 continues to be routed through the middle of Richardson Grove on a two-lane roadway dating back to the 1910s.

For those who did stop and see the redwoods, Chapin recommended Richardson Grove, with its many amenities. One attraction that Chapin highlighted was a fallen tree that had been cut so that the growth rings could be seen. The tree had fallen four years earlier and had been turned into an interpretive device, pointing to the age of the tree and how earlier damage done to the tree had not killed it. Important dates in man's history were marked on the log, with Chapin noting, "In its more than 1200 years of existence this tree has lived through some of the most stirring and significant events in the history of the human race."[153]

Another controversy to strike against Richardson Grove in 1937 was the park commission wanting to reopen a restaurant there. The Humboldt County Board of Supervisors was opposed, as it felt that the restaurant would be in competition with local businesses and that the park's purpose was to protect and preserve the redwoods. The supervisors felt, "If the state park commission established a general policy of commercializing state recreational property in competition with private enterprise, it would

After falling due to old age, this section was cut out of the tree and used to highlight the age of the tree. *CSPA.*

107

result in bankruptcy of hundreds of present resort owners. Establishing a restaurant would be a decidedly bad precedent."[154] Causing concern was the granting of concession to L.A. Spangler to operate the cabins, store and other facilities at Richardson Grove, similar to the one granted to Edwin Freeman. Freeman had returned to the Bay Area in the late 1930s, dying in 1939. Beyond condemning the practice, the board "adopted a resolution urging that all commercial business at Richardson Grove be immediately discontinued and that the cabins and all other equipment used commercially in said grove be immediately removed."[155] The State Parks Commission listened to concerns of the Redwood Empire Association and the county's but took no action at its meeting in 1939. William Kenyon was the state park ranger assigned to Richardson Grove that year.

In 1939, Harriet Weaver, who was the first female ranger for the California state park system, came to work at Richardson Grove. She started working at Big Basin in 1929. During World War II, she served in the Women's Ambulance and Defense Corps. She returned to ranger work at Big Basin, retiring in 1974. During the summer she spent at Richardson Grove, she found herself very busy. Her day was captured by Dick Bergholz in 1940:

At 7 o'clock, the state warden's office opens and registrations begin for campers and tourists. For about eight solid hours she is a combination office worker and human encyclopedia—she has to spot license numbers from all 48 states, has to know the answers to questions ranging from "Why do you burn your trees [in forest fires] *in California?" to "What is the tallest tree in the park?"*

In the afternoon she becomes a one-woman first aid crew, treating stubbed toes, scratched knees and slivered fingers. She acts as a sort of assistant life guard at the park swimming beach on Eel River.

She also has the important job of being park hostess—introducing the lady from Oshkosh, Michigan to her neighbor in the tent down the path who comes to the park every year from Tucson, Ariz. She has to see to it that the elderly couple from Texas get a quiet campsite away from the nocturnal noise of the dancehall, that the trailer family from Missouri are located near some other similar midwestern family.

And because state law provides that dogs in Richardson grove must be kept on a leash, she becomes a one-woman dog-catching crew, rounding up the strays and returning dogs to their owners.

At night, after a full day of hustle and work Miss Weaver becomes a "recreational director" by conducting the big daily campfire circles. Here

Right: Harriet Weaver, the first female ranger in California State Parks, worked at Richardson Grove helping visitors learn about the redwoods. *Fillmore Historical Museum.*

Below: Campfire programs remain a staple of evenings in the state parks, and campers share in songs and skits and learn about the region. *CPHLSC.*

she leads singing, tells stories, digs up amateur talent of any quantity or quality. There are usually from 2000–3000 persons in the grove and at least 800–1000 attend the campfire circles. Many times she's had to beg, borrow or steal entertainment talent of some sort, but she's never failed to put on at least a 90-minute program.

After the campfire circles nightly from 7:30 to 9:30, Miss Weaver goes over to the lodge where card games and indoor amusements are conducted, and to the dance hall where young and old dance to the nickelodeon from 9:30 to 11 p.m.

Then things are quieted down in the park—by state law—and in a few more hours of patrolling and general duty, Miss Weaver's day comes to a sleepy end.

Many who have worked as rangers or park aides for the California Park system recognize multiple aspects of this day in the park.

World War II curtailed trips to the redwoods; however, when the war ended, the campgrounds again filled with campers. To accommodate the renewed visitation, park staff revamped both their water and sewage system in 1947. The park reinstituted dances the following year, and soon all the entertainments that attracted visitors in the past were in full swing. The park also added longer parking spurs at this time to meet the needs of the increasing number of trailers being towed to the park. The early 1950s appeared to have Richardson Grove returned to the days of Freeman. However, the 1955 December flood caused significant damage to the park's campgrounds and trails. Notes from the rangers on staff captured the event: "December 22, water up to eaves of houses, all houses and contents ruined from the flood. No lights, power, phone, or water. Road full of slides. It [the floodwaters] twisted and demolished buildings, buried campsites with silt and caused siltation of the grove. Thirty-five ancient trees were lost within the park."[156] The rangers had no place to escape the floodwaters, except higher ground; the road was closed to the north and south. In January, Bob Skamser, a reporter for the *Santa Rosa Press Democrat*, managed to get north to Humboldt County to cover the damage. When he reached Richardson Grove, he found that "the main buildings near the highway were intact. Roadside and park garbage cans were piled high with muddy personal belongings of the park ranger crew....Near the bank of the Eel River a black top road led up to where a neat group of ranger homes had been, surrounded by a large expanse of lawn. This is all gone now."[157] The damage to the park caused campsites to be relocated, while many of the camp stoves

Campers in the 1950s and '60s found more campsites, enjoying hiking the trails and swimming in the river. *CSPA.*

built by the CCC were buried under three to four feet of silt. The state park commission also took the opportunity to not rebuild the cabins ruined by the flood. While this angered some, it helped the park slowly pull back from having so many concessions and become less of a resort destination, although the campgrounds continue to attract thousands to the park as a destination for campers. The change also reflected the changes in values of campers. Many wanted more of an outdoor experience, or they brought what they needed in their own trailers.

In 1959, Richardson Grove opened the summer season with the new facilities. These included "a highway underpass, an improved water system, an improved electrical system, a communication system, six comfort stations, [bathroom and sinks], two combination buildings [shower and bathrooms], a new area office, a residence and service building, a 700 person seating capacity campfire center, surfaced roads, and parking lots, eighty new camp units, twelve summer help quarters and a new checking station." The underpass made traveling to the day-use area and campgrounds across the river safer. The campsites were also away from the old-growth forest, where

Richardson Grove, although no longer a resort, remains a popular destination for campers. *CSPA.*

the campers had innocently caused damage to the trees' fragile roots by walking and parking on them.[158] The new alignment allowed for 18 day-use sites and 184 campsites. The new facilities were well received by the public, with the grove seeing 371,289 visitors in 1960, 61,958 of whom camped at the park.[159] Another change brought about the flood was the closure of the store and restaurant at the grove. However, in 1962 a concession was granted to allow operation of the store, and patrons could purchase food, gifts and souvenirs. The store also featured a soda fountain.

While the 1964 flood was much more devastating for the redwoods and facilities for Humboldt Redwoods State Park, it was less so for Richardson Grove. The rangers were again isolated, but with the moving of the residences away from the river, there was less damage to facilities. In April 1965, the grove had thirty-six sites open, with another thirty-eight planned to be open by the summer season. Additionally, ninety-four of the sites across the river at Oak Flats would be opened as staff had been able to repair the flood-damaged water system.

A constant since its opening is Richardson Grove's popularity with the public. Thousands are attracted over summer months, with locals and tourists alike enjoying swimming, camping and hiking among the tall trees. The park has grown to 1,771 acres, 171 campsites and eleven miles of hiking trails. A visitor center was opened in the 1990s in the old store building, which was remodeled in the 2010s.

Chapter 4

PRAIRIE CREEK STATE PARK

The year 1923 saw the start of Prairie Creek Redwoods State Park, north of the small community of Orick. Prairie Creek began with a donation of 166 acres of redwood forestland by local large landowner Zipporah Russ. Her family had owned a mill in Eureka, as well as ranch lands west and east of the Eel River, near Ferndale, California. Like the tall groves of redwoods along the South Fork of the Eel River, the trees in Northern Humboldt were also far from the mills closer to Humboldt Bay. The groves began to be protected at the same time they became vulnerable to logging with trucks. In fact, the small town of Orick south of the park was based on the timber industry. The efforts of the Save the Redwoods League can be seen in this park, filled with groves of redwood, hemlock and fir. The park has grown to be one of the popular redwood state parks.

Zipporah Russ immigrated to California in 1852 with her family, settling in the rich farmlands along the Eel River. Her husband, Joseph Russ, came to California in 1850 and drove a herd of cattle to Humboldt County in 1852. Russ settled in the Bear River region of the county, at one point owning fifty thousand acres of land. In 1872, he was part owner of the Excelsior Lumber Mill, located on Gunther Island in Humboldt Bay. He also served as a state assemblyman. He and Zipporah married in 1854, when she was sixteen. Zipporah and her family had arrived in California three years earlier, having crossed the Great Plains from Illinois. The couple had thirteen children. Russ died in 1886, but his wife and children continued to operate the many aspects of his business.[160] Before he died, Russ became

Prairie Creek State Park began in 1923 and has grown to become one of the most popular of the Redwood State Parks. *HRIA.*

involved in a scheme to purchase large stands of redwoods in Northern Humboldt. Taking advantage of the homestead laws, he and his partners had individuals file a patent for a 160-acre homestead, and after purchasing the land, the patent filers turned around and sold it to Russ's consortium. In this way, large swaths of land came under his ownership. When the scheme was discovered, the land, and the Excelsior Mill operated by Russ, were sold off, bought up by the Sage Land and Improvement Company. This group also purchased land from Hammond Lumber Company and Little River Lumber Company. Zipporah Russ and her sons ably managed all of the remaining Russ interests. Zipporah remaining active in many community groups. She was involved in campaigning to secure the right to vote for women. In addition to donating land to the Save the Redwoods League, she also gave land to the City of Ferndale and to the State of California.[161]

By the early 1920s, Zipporah Russ had become involved in the many meetings held about the need to preserve the redwoods; she was influenced in her decision, according to the *Ferndale Enterprise,* by her daughter Georgia Williams, who also lived in Ferndale. Her husband, Frank Williams, was president of the Russ-Williams Banking Company. Mrs. Williams was known for her interest in the efforts of the Save the Redwoods League, writing several poems "expressing her keen interest in the preservation of these mightiest of trees." One of her poems expressed her "strong regret over the destruction of the redwoods":

> *Today they are cutting the Redwoods,*
> *Cutting the beautiful trees*
> *I can hear no sound in the world*
> *But the cry of the falling trees*
> *From the groves on the rich river levels*
> *Where stood they since ages long gone*
> *To the tops of the high-crested mountains*
> *They mow ruthlessly,*
> *Steadily on.*[162]

The grove that Mrs. Russ donated to the Save the Redwoods League was described by Herbert Briggs, editor of the *Ferndale Enterprise,* as follows:

> *The tract contains 166 acres and has a stand of close to thirty million feet of redwood, as well as much other timber. It is admirably situated on the State Highway above Orick and is crossed diagonally by Prairie Creek,*

Right: Zipporah Russ took over the family business interests when her husband died in 1886. In 1923, she donated redwood lands starting Prairie Creek State Park. *HHS*.

Below: A *Ferndale Enterprise* editor noted that Russ grove, with "the redwoods…together with the giant ferns and other undergrowth make it an area of unusual beauty." *HRIA*.

a good sized stream that adds to the beauty of the grove....Some of the largest trees of the redwood belt are found on this tract of timber....Not only the redwoods, but also the massive firs, hemlocks, maples, spruce, oaks and other trees found in this tract, together with the giant ferns and other undergrowth make it an area of unusual beauty. It is still in its primeval state, and many of its acres have probably never been trodden by man.[163]

A unique aspect of the new park was the fact that a herd of Roosevelt elk resided in the area and continue to do so. The herd was described in 1932 in the *Stockton Evening and Sunday Record*. The paper explained, "Another interesting feature of the park is the herd of Roosevelt Elk which roams between the Prairie Creek and the ocean." The paper reminded readers that the elk were nearing extinction in California, a fate that had been met by the grizzly bear and condor in the state. In 1932, there were only three hundred head of elk left in the state, all of them in the herd north of Orick. The paper further explained, "These timid and gentle creatures are seldom seen in daylight, but may be noted occasionally emerging from the forest and wandering along the ocean beach." It was the hope of the paper that "the park may become a sanctuary for these elk, where they may be adequately protected from man and beast." Ultimately, the paper observed, "To many the friendliness and fearlessness of the native animals in our national and State parks which have been protected all their lives, is one of the inspiring features to be found in these preserves."[164] Sighting of elk at Prairie Creek has become a highlight of any visit to the region.

With the donation of the Pioneer Grove, the Save the Redwoods League began working to enlarge the park. In 1925, the SRL added the Roberts Claim to the new park. The Humboldt County Board of Supervisors "voted $40,000 to purchase this second-tract."[165] By 1932, four thousand acres, mostly from the Sage Land Improvement Company, had been added to the initial land. With the start of the Depression, the company found cash inflow more vital than land. The park was named as a whole after the large meadow or prairie that elk roamed in, next to the redwoods. Prior to the park, the area was simply known as "The Prairie," with the state adding the creek to the name, giving it the name it has been known as since then, Prairie Creek Redwoods State Park.[166]

Despite economic hardships of the Great Depression, the *San Francisco Examiner* encouraged visitors in 1932 to explore the park, which differed from the groves in Southern Humboldt due to its mixture of other types of timber. Frank Lyman, automobile editor for the *Examiner*, encouraged travelers by

ELK AT PRAIRIE CREEK STATE PARK, 6 M NORTH OF ORICK
© 1941 by E. Hess   REDWOOD HIGHWAY, CALIFORNIA   L9

The Roosevelt elk herd at Prairie Creek was all that was left of these members of the deer family in California when the park was created. *HRIA.*

describing Prairie Creek as one "of the most majestic gems in the diadem of California's wonders taking rank with Yosemite, the beaches and the great river and forest areas of the High Sierra."[167] Lyman also believed that anyone traveling to the Olympic Games in Los Angeles that year should stop and enjoy the park. Lyman observed, "Californians who never have seen these coast redwoods in their full splendor owe it to themselves as citizens of the state to view them, and a trip to Prairie Creek State Redwoods should be on the vacation itinerary."[168]

As with the parks in Southern Humboldt, the Civilian Conservation Corps was a boon for Prairie Creek Redwoods. A CCC camp was established near Orick, at Prairie Creek. The men worked extensively in the park. The *Humboldt Times* explained the challenges faced by men who were implementing the CCC in the county:

> *The battle front against depression in the Eureka district of the Civilian Conservation Corps, commanded by Lieut. Col. L.L. Pendleton, C.A.C., covers as much territory as the entire western front during the World War. From north to south, the district extends 400 miles and from west to east by airline about 80 miles. However, the distance by negotiable roads is much greater and from headquarters in Eureka to the various camps*

CCC Camp Company 1903, near Orick, was established in 1933. The men built trails, campsites and some buildings at Prairie Creek State Park. *CPHLSC.*

ranged from 45 to 270 miles....Two camps are on paved highways and another only a few hundred yards away, but the other six are reached by roads that give to the traveler the combined thrill of a rollercoaster and airplane, hedge hopping.[169]

Similar to the camp at Dyerville, the men worked on erosion control and built trails, campsites, camp stoves and other projects around the park. They also had to build their own cabins and buildings, completed in 1933.[170] One project was to build a campfire center. The stage was built between two redwoods. One man, Robert Spray, had a different assignment; he was hired by the CCC as an artist to "paint and sketch the work of the Civilian Conservation Corps in the country's State parks." Spray's artwork was displayed in San Diego in 1935 in a "special CCC exhibition at the Pacific International Exposition. The paintings of Spray included vivid and realistic portraits of camp projects and landscapes in the immediate vicinity."[171] Similarly, another Bay Area artist, James McCray, was sent to Dyerville to capture images of the men stationed there.

Newton Drury came with Colonel Wing, director of the State Parks, to inspect the new camp at Prairie Creek. Drury was quoted in the *Humboldt Times*: "The work being done in state parks by the Civilian Conservation Corps is of outstanding benefit with the developments being accomplished which would have many years to complete." The *Times* further reported, "The three men were profuse in their praise of the new construction, under the direction of First Lt. Edwin P. Crandall, 11th Cavalry, and Capt. Mark Thomas, F.A. Res., including the landscaping of the camp under the direction of Mr. Meyers."[172] While most of the men stationed at the CCC camp near Prairie Creek were from the region, one young man, Walter Nelson, was from Redwood Valley, near Ukiah. He worked at the camp for ten months, receiving "special mention in the form of increased wages and a certificate of leadership, making him assistant leader of the camp." Nelson later returned to Redwood Valley to work at a local store.[173]

The CCC camp newspaper at Prairie Creek, the *Prairie Creek Prattle*, covered work done by company 1903. In the October 26, 1934 edition, the editors covered some of the projects underway. One trail made went from "the Big Tree, parallels the highway and meets the Brown Creek Trail. This trail is of particular interest because of the giant trees one sees along it. The crew discovered a tree larger than the Big Tree while building the new trail."[174] In addition to being able to take literacy classes at Prairie Creek, in 1934 the men were also able to take a business course. Other classes offered included a discussion class and a slide rule class. The camp also featured a library.

In July 1935, the camp received seventeen new men from Crescent City to help build trails. Additionally, ninety-three men from Oakland and San Francisco arrived to bring the camp up to full capacity. In November, the men learned about the historical uses of the park from Mr. C.A. Boyes, one of the state park foremen and son of the man who the area was first named after. Boyes explained:

> *Boyes Prairie was quite a rendezvous for the Indians living on the Klamath river. They preferred the salmon found in Prairie Creek to those found in the Klamath. Moreover, elk, deer, and bear were so plentiful that frequent trips were made to Boyes Prairie for fish and game. Following its development we find Boyes Prairie the scene of a deadly feud for its possession; it is overrun by prospectors when gold was found at the Bluffs. It is turned into a prosperous farm by Mr. Boyes; a wagon road is built to transport supplies and then an interstate highway passes through; the government takes an*

option on the prairie and today we find Prairie Creek CCC camp located on this historical site.[175]

In 1936, an additional 40 acres of redwood lands were added to the park through purchase from the State Park Bonds. The following year, another 160 acres were added. This added land not only protected the redwoods but also added protected range for the Roosevelt elk in the area. The State Parks hoped to create a refuge for the elk to keep them safe. By 1941, taking care of the elk had "become a full time job" and a priority for the state park according to Kenneth Fulton, state director of natural resources. Fulton shared to the United Press that "many travelers report the elk are as great an attraction as the redwoods in that area....There are approximately 200 elk in the park and the adjacent area and during the tourist season the biggest problem is to keep visitors from bothering elk in the Elk Prairie, a mile-long area bisected by the highway."[176] The park continues to protect and manage the elk, even at times sending some to other parks to help rebuild some of their historic range. In 1961, some of the elk were sent to other parks, but rounding them up proved to be challenging. Roping was not successful, so stuffing apples with tranquilizers was tried instead; this was found to be a successful way to move the animals.[177] Managing the herd is one of the challenging duties for park staff.

The elk at Prairie Creek State Park have been protected and managed to maintain the herd's health; sometimes this includes allowing hunting of the animals. *HRIA.*

During World War II, in 1943, a proposal was made by the U.S. Department of Agriculture to "remove 30,000,000 board feet of lumber in Prairie Creek Humboldt State Park for manufacture of boxes and crates."[178] The boxes were needed in shipping supplies oversees to Armed Forces. There was a critical need, thus "the lumber [was] removed under jurisdiction of the War Production Board [which] will relieve pressing need for boxes and crates essential to movement of material for the nation's fighting forces." Indeed, the need was so great that 30 million board feet was "cut during the remainder of the year in the northern California forests." The state park board also authorized "use of two access roads for movement of men, materials, and lumber."[179]

Following the war, another proposal was put forth to create a Redwood National Park by U.S. Assemblywoman Helen Gahagan Douglas. Her proposal called for a series of four national parks starting near the Oregon border and extending south to Richardson Grove. Her second memorial unit "about 35,000 acres in Northern Humboldt county, takes in most of the Prairie Creek drainage to the ocean shore [Gold Bluffs] south nearly to Orick."[180] Prairie Creek State Park falls within this unit. Douglas wanted to dedicate the park in memory of Franklin D. Roosevelt. However, she ran into stiff resistance, as her bill would remove 367,500 acres from the tax rolls and, of course, a great deal of privately owned land from logging. She tried again to pass the bill, but it failed as well.

Despite opposition to the larger national park, smaller purchases through the auspices of the Save the Redwoods League and memorial grove program continued to be made. The Soroptimist International Clubs began raising money to purchase a grove in "Prairie Creek state park contain[ing] seven million feet of standing redwood" in 1946. The grove cost the organization $10,000.[181] Similarly, the Garden Clubs of America again were raising money, this time to purchase a grove in Prairie Creek. The Garden Club was able to purchase a 40-acre parcel to add to the park. The Rotary Clubs of California also engaged in fundraising, purchasing a grove adding to Prairie Creek. Indeed, between 1945 and 1948, the State Department of Natural Resources spent $47,366 for additions to Prairie Creek.[182] During that time, it also had a residence and shops built for the ranger stationed at the park. In January 1948, the Save the Redwoods League gave the state $76,000 to purchase 220 acres of redwood land near Prairie Creek.[183] Its donation was matched by the state; the 220 acres along with 1,380 already in the park were renamed the Madison Grant Forest and Elk Reserve.[184] Another memorial grove dedicated in 1948 was the Earl Warren Grove, in honor of

A campsite at Prairie Creek Campground features table and chairs, as well as a camp stove built by the CCC workers. *HRIA.*

California's then governor, who later became the fourteenth chief justice of the Supreme Court. Groves added in the 1950s include those dedicated to Frederick Olmsted, Luther Burbank and C.A. Schenck. The California Real Estate Association also donated money for a memorial grove. Through the memorial grove program and matching state funds, by 1955 the park had grown to 10,000 acres.

In 1952, Matthew Rice described Prairie Creek for the *Humboldt Standard* as having one hundred campsites and ten day-use areas. Additionally, he felt that it was "outstanding for its primeval forest growths…grocery store, nature guide service, fire circle, curio shop, fishing, [and]…50 miles of trails."[185] Rice noted that the park included the elk preserve, protecting the only remaining elk herd in California. He alerted visitors that elk "may be seen on both sides of the highway." The year 1953 saw the addition of Fern Canyon to Prairie Creek State Park. Part of the Home Creek watershed, the canyon is unique—a narrow, "vertical-walled canyon, thirty feet or more deep…its sides are covered with myriads of the rare and delicate five-fingered ferns."[186] Endangered by potential logging in the area, the rarity was preserved that summer. The state spent $500,000 to purchase the land around the canyon and four miles of beachfront.[187] This stretch of land proved difficult to acquire, as the state moved to use condemnation of land for public good against The Pacific Lumber Company to acquire it. Fortunately, the state was able to protect the canyon. Following its acquisition, a small campground, Gold Bluffs Beach, was added to the park facilities in 1968. Fern Canyon and Gold Bluffs Beach have grown in popularity, the canyon becoming one of the best-known hikes in Prairie Creek.

Gold Bluffs Beach forms a unique part of Prairie Creek State Park as well. Site of a minor gold rush in the early 1850s, it didn't last, as the sand particles were so minute. In 1873, the *San Francisco Examiner* noted "very rich deposits are said to exist on the coast.…The first discovery…was made at Gold Bluff."[188] The previous year, a bell submarine tried to extract the gold. In 1872, John Chapman "formed the Union Gold Bluff Placer Mine with himself as the superintendent and principal owner. It was during the period between 1872 and 1901…that the lower bluff claim produced substantial amounts of gold."[189] It was claimed in 1881 that the amount of treasure "taken from the two claims runs into the millions."[190] A flume was built to bring water to the operations from Prairie Creek in 1888. In 1892, the gold was assayed as being "from 900 to 950 fine and sells for $19.50 an ounce."[191] The company was purchased in 1902 and also engaged in logging at that time. The Gold Bluff Mining and Logging Company employed fifty-two men that year. The next year, it employed a dredger at the mine site. The Miner Ridge trail at Prairie Creek follows the miners' path to the Gold Bluff's camp. A gold extraction plant was put to use at the Lower Bluff operations in 1913. At one point, a tunnel was dug to add in the gold extraction.

State Park Ranger Sam Rich, unit ranger at Gold Bluff Beach from March 1984 until January 1991, was very interested in the tunnel:

The tunnel was something I had found while doing the unit's history. There was a short article about the gold being mined in the late 1800s along the bluffs during low tide near the mouth of Fern Canyon. An idea was suggested that if a better source of flowing water was available during high tides, more sand could be put through the process of removing the gold flakes. A tunnel was proposed to come from the east, where water flowed from Prairie Creek, taking it through the hills at the shortest distance across to Gold Bluffs Beach. The article said the tunnel hadn't been dug correctly, as water wouldn't flow westward at that point and was abandoned. I had found a hand drawn map showing a tunnel as described. I talked with the late Ranger Terry Adams who had been in the area a long time. He said he remembered the tunnel being a problem with kids partying and homeless living at the mouth of the tunnel on the east side. Terry said the decision

This 1880s sketch depicts mining operations at Gold Beach. While many walked away empty-handed, the mine produced some $2 million in bullion. *CPHLSC.*

was to have Cal Trans dynamite the tunnel. Ranger John Melvin was the one who located what we believe to have been the former east side mouth of tunnel. I went out there with him and you could see a pool of water at the base of the hill. Prairie Creek was off to the side and it looked like a short channel had been dug to the pool. There was a large number of unnatural rock piles to the north side. At the base we both saw water seeping out, back toward Prairie Creek. I went back out with the late Maintenance Worker Karl Knapp to see if we could locate the west entrance. Starting at the east side we worked our way with machetes straight up and over to the west side along Gold Bluffs Beach. The terrain was heavily covered with down[ed] trees and plant foliage. Unfortunately, we were unsuccessful in locating the west side entrance.[192]

The 1955 flood that caused extensive damage to Humboldt Redwoods and Richardson Grove State Parks did little damage to Prairie Creek. Located away from a major river, it saw little damage but did provide a refuge for some residents of Orick, which was threatened by rising waters from Redwood Creek. Prairie Creek was one of the few state parks in Humboldt County to be fully operational in 1956, attracting even more visitors as the Southern Humboldt parks focused on recovery. In fact, Prairie Creek had an "increase of over 100%" for the 1956 tourist season.[193] In 1958, 216,000 visitors stopped at the park. Summer months were also popular times to

Newton Drury (*center*) and Governor Brown (*seated*) look over proposals to build a freeway near Prairie Creek State Park. *CSPA.*

have grove dedications at Prairie Creek. The years between 1955 and 1965 continued to see many groves acquired and dedicated. Former California governor Frank Merriam was honored with a grove in 1959. That same year, another grove was dedicated to Robert Sproul, president emeritus of University of California–Berkley, and his wife. More land was purchased that year when Mrs. James Van Lobensels donated $14,000 to the SRL for a grove to honor her husband at Prairie Creek. In 1961, the Edward G. Schmitedell grove was approved by the State Park Commission.

A new controversy came to Prairie Creek in 1964, caused by the same issues that affected the groves along the South Fork of the Eel. Visitors to the northern region of the county were in competition with logging trucks, residents and other travelers for space on the road. Several fatal car wrecks demonstrated the dangers of the narrow road winding through the redwoods. The solution sought by the Division of Roads and Highways was to build a four-lane freeway, much as it had been building along the parklands of Southern Humboldt. Of the proposals offered, one was for a highway built alongside the ocean, across what is now one of the few wilderness beaches in the state. Another plan had the freeway built on the bluffs above the beach, while a third had the highway routed through logged-over lands to the east of the park. The beach and Fern Canyon had not yet been purchased by the state. Adding to the controversy was the proposal made by Lyndon B. Johnson for a redwood national park that would encompass Prairie Creek State Park and an additional fifty-three thousand acres of timber. The SRL had long been a proponent of a redwood national park, and by the end of the decade, the new park had been established. The flood of 1964, although not affecting Prairie Creek directly, redirected funds and efforts away from Prairie Creek to repair damage done to parks and roads in the southern portion of the county. Highways were severely damaged, with sixteen bridges on the state highway washed away, including the large bridge over the Klamath River just to the north of the park. Large slides also washed away extensive sections of highway. As a result, money that might have been used to build the redwood bypass in the 1960s was used in reopening the entire route of 101 in Northern California. The four-lane freeway built east of Prairie Creek was not completed until 1992. Redwood trees cut down to make way for the freeway were hauled to various California missions to be used to repair those structures.

In 1965, the Save the Redwoods League completed the purchase of Fern Canyon, which had been described by the National Park Service as "a unique and fragile jewel,"[194] and other forestland from The Pacific Lumber Company. The total acreage purchased was 2,095 and was the result of long negotiations. Earlier in May of that year, a condemnation suit was pursued to purchase the land, but The Pacific Lumber Company, the state and the Save the Redwoods League were able to reach a settlement. Significantly, the purchase not only protected Fern Canyon but also provided access from

Young Kimberly Nichols plays in her campsite at Gold Bluff's Beach; the campground sits where the proposed freeway would have navigated the coast. *Author image.*

Prairie Creek to the beach, which was also now protected by the state. The addition expanded Prairie Creek to 12,423 acres.

As the number of memorial groves grew and word spread about the beautiful groves of trees to be found in Prairie Creek, interest in the area as a location for filming movies also grew. The earliest movie filmed in the area was 1936's *The Last of the Mohicans*, starring Randolph Scott. Twenty local Yurok Native Americans played the roles of the Mohicans. The year 1952 saw Kirk Douglas filming *The Big Trees*. This film used footage shot at Williams Grove as well as Prairie Creek.[195] In the 1990s, several blockbuster movies were filmed in the redwood groves of Prairie Creek. In 1995, Johnny Depp filmed *Dead Man*, a twist on the more traditional western. Fern Canyon made its cinematic debut in 1997's *The Lost World*. The narrow canyon lined with ferns was seen again two years later in *Walking with Dinosaurs*. Images of Prairie Creek along with Grizzly Creek State Park are found in 2011's *The Tree of Life*, starring Brad Pitt.

Prairie Creek remains a popular state park, protecting 13,832 acres of forestland, with 101 campsites and seventy-seven miles of trails. A visitor center welcomes travelers to the park, housed in a building built by the CCC in the 1930s. With the redwood bypass completed in 1993, the original highway was renamed the Newton B. Drury Parkway. The parkway provides

Fern Canyon is a unique site, as the canyon walls are covered with many varieties of fern; it was featured in the documentary *Walking with Dinosaurs*. *CSPA*.

access to the campground and, like the Avenue of the Giants, is a scenic alternate to the four-lane freeway. Newton Drury was involved with the Save the Redwoods League almost from its inception and served as chairman, secretary and commissioner. He was also a director for the California State Parks and director for the National Park Service. During his lifetime, Drury

The redwoods at Prairie Creek along the Newton Drury Parkway, December 2022. *Author image.*

was instrumental in raising $25 million in donations for the preservation of 135,000 acres of redwoods.[196] Drury received many accolades for the work he had done for the state and national parks. He has groves named for him, but perhaps this drive through the primeval forest is the one that best honors his efforts on behalf of future generations to enjoy the redwoods.

Chapter 5

DEL NORTE REDWOODS AND
JEDEDIAH SMITH REDWOODS

Isolated from the rest of the state by the terrain and rivers that bisected the coastal mountains, Del Norte County interests were focused around the county seat at Crescent City. One mill dominated the lumber business for the first sixty years of Euro-American settlement, the Hobbes-Wall Company. Started in the 1880s, the company was active in the box manufacturing trade and thus more interested in logging hemlock and spruce trees than redwoods. The other conifers were smaller, easier to manage and able to be shipped from the port at Crescent City. The company operated two mills, one at Lake Earl and one in Elk Valley. By 1919, the company was also operating three logging camps and a company store in Crescent City. It also boasted of a twelve-mile railroad line completed in 1894. Its operations began to expand toward Howland Hill in 1908. During World War I, the company harvested spruce for airplane manufacture. The company closed its operations in 1939. Following World War II, logging surged, with bulldozers, more powerful chainsaws and trucks hauling logs. By 1954, "there were 40 logging, lumber and plywood operations in the county....The annual timber harvest zoomed from 53,000,000 in 1946 to 300,000,000 in 1953."[197] It was at this time that the Save the Redwoods League become involved in purchasing as much land as it could to protect the redwoods.

Del Norte Redwoods started with the donation of several groves to SRL in 1925. When the redwood groves in Del Norte County were purchased, whether along the coast or along the Smith River (named after American explorer Jedediah Smith), they were all given the appellation of Del Norte

SCENE AT CRESCENT CITY, CALIFORNIA.

The steep land around Crescent City is shown in this picture of Damnation Creek. This region is now protected in public lands. *CPHLSC.*

Redwoods, as a group. The first redwoods donated were groves located on steep hillsides extending from ocean beaches to mountain crest. The first grove protected was a donation by George Schwarz, who purchased 157 acres he donated to the state in honor of Henry S. Graves, former chief forester for the United States. Schwarz gave an additional 260 acres to the park, these lands also on the steep coast. More land was purchased or donated around the original Graves Grove until the park within a short six years had reached 2,300 acres. In 1928, a small 20-acre tract of land was preserved when it was learned that "the tract of land which harbors a large grove of redwoods was owned by a company that contemplated cutting the timber, $5,500 was raised and the property purchased....The tract is the first piece of timberland reached on the...highway."[198] J.D. Grant, one of the founders of the SR, also added to Del Norte Redwoods with a memorial grove in 1929.[199] Another 640 acres were donated that same

Stout Grove, on the south side of Smith River, is one of the groves that form Jedediah Smith State Park. *HRIA.*

year in honor of George Knapp of Santa Barbara.[200] These groves were remote and inaccessible, in very steep terrain, with the groves stretching from the ocean to 1,100 feet in elevation. As a result, these groves saw little attention or interest for several years.

In 1929, Stout Memorial Grove was added to Del Norte Redwoods. This popular grove is located some five miles east of Crescent City, on the south side of the Smith River. The grove includes "44 acres of remarkable timber at the mouth of Mill Creek, where it enters the Smith River."[201] This grove was donated by Clara Stout in honor of her husband, Frank D. Stout, who had been a lumberman in Northern California. It formed the nucleus of what is now known as Jedediah Smith State Park. It soon became an objective of the Save the Redwoods League to acquire all of the Mill Creek watershed, to protect the redwoods found along the creek.

Part of the reason the Del Norte redwoods remained relatively unknown was because from the south, access was via a ferry crossing the Klamath River near the community of Klamath. The ferry discouraged many from going farther north. The *Stockton Independent* explained that the ferry's "operation is suspended by high water in the winter and low water in summer, which frequently closes off Del Norte County from the remainder of the state, except by ocean voyage."[202] Then, in 1926, the Douglas Memorial Bridge was completed and decorated with four gold painted grizzly bear statues. However, many drivers were still intimidated by the curvy roads leading into Del Norte County. The park also consisted only of the preserved land, as there were no trails or camping facilities. Helping the park gain in popularity was an article in the 1931 *Sierra Club Bulletin* by Emerson Knight about the novel redwood state park on the ocean cliff. Knight advised readers:

> *This park, comprising an area of 2300 acres, is noteworthy for its topography ranging from sea level to 1100 feet upward, its rich variety in flora and fauna and its wealth of impressive scenic beauty....The park is unique on account of its redwood forest of stately gigantic trees on steep slopes, being closely related to the dramatic broken shore line in constant state of evolution below. The Graves Grove of redwoods lying in the very heart of this park is an area of most extraordinary beauty.*[203]

Knight submitted a report to the SRL advocating for the park to be about three thousand acres, although he believed that the park could be expanded further. Knight had helped to scout out the one trail constructed in the park. The trail was intriguing to hike, winding through three zones, with

The steep transition between coastland and redwood forest between the Del Norte County line and Crescent City. *CSPA.*

thick redwood followed by a less dense region of alders and other deciduous trees. Finally, the trail reached the beach, the last zone of the trail. Knight described the scene: "As far as the eye can penetrate dim mists of distance, ridge on ridge descend in rhythmic order to become one with the ocean." Also helping to attract visitors was the park being listed as thirty-second out of fifty-eight "interesting places to visit" in 1931 by the *Sacramento Bee.*[204]

More trails were built during the 1930s as Del Norte Redwoods was enhanced through the efforts of the Civilian Conservation Corps men stationed at Crescent City. Similarly to other parks, state park employees worked closely with the CCC officials and men, with all following plans being laid out by park personnel. Little remains of work done by the CCC,

Mill Creek Redwoods, near the mouth of the creek, was the first state campground in Del Norte County. *HRIA.*

except for the trails the workers built. The CCC also improved trails and access into Stout Grove. CCC Company 709 near Gasquet was one of the camps open year round. The CCC crews helped fight wildfires in the area, and in 1937 "members of Camp Gasquet learned that a woman with a small baby was surrounded by fire seven miles back in the hills. The youths found flames up to the yard fence on all sides, but plunged in and saved the house and both lives, although they were forced to run a flaming gauntlet for two miles along a mountain road."[205] Their efforts also helped to protect the redwoods along the Smith. Some of the men involved in the rescue were from Humboldt County.

In 1935, the *Santa Rosa Republican* decided to answer the questions of "How many parks and points of interest are included in the California state park system? Where are they located? What forms of recreation?" The paper arranged with the State Park Commission to print the list of coastal parks. Del Norte Redwoods was described as a "magnificent area [which] is on the Redwood Highway about 10 miles south of Crescent City. It affords an unusual contrast between the forest and the sea inasmuch as the redwoods grow on rolling slopes which rise from the ocean. The western boundary of the park extends along 7 miles of ocean shore. There are good trails along which rhododendrons bloom profusely in late May or early June."

To distinguish between parcels of redwood parklands, the groves along the Smith River were referred to as "Hiouchi Redwoods." They were described as containing "virgin redwood forest of the northern type with a heavy growth of ferns and other undergrowth. One of the features is the Stout Grove of unusually big trees on the old Highway south of Crescent City."[206]

In 1941, the *San Francisco Examiner* urged the state legislature to appropriate funds for purchase of groves along the Smith River for a park, noting that "it has taken some of these trees 2,000 years to reach their present magnificence. A tree could be cut down and reduced to fence rails in 2,000 minutes." Furthermore, "this appropriation is computed as one fiftieth of 1 percent of the State budget." The paper therefore believed that "the legislature should consider it is not betraying any economy ideal by 'saving the redwoods!'"[207] In 1942, the SRL matched funds with the State of California to purchase a "parcel of Mill Creek Redwoods."[208] Mill Creek's watershed flows from the south, flowing into Smith River near Stout Grove. The five thousand acres purchased was near Stout Grove and the mouth of Mill Creek. In 1947, the grove was added to the Hiouchi park and dedicated as the National Tribute Grove, honoring those who served and are serving in war. The *Oakland Tribune* observed, "Ever-living redwoods, the oldest of growing things, are to stand through the years to come and, in the majesty and silence of their enduring companionship will honor the men and women of the armed services of the United States in World War II."[209] Dedicated in 1949, the grove has the distinction of being the largest living memorial to the soldiers of World War II. Helping with the fundraising were several organizations, including the Soroptimists International, the Garden Clubs of America and Daughters of the American Revolution. At the dedication, Newton Drury described the grove as "ever-living 'memorial of eternal gratitude, eternally expressed' to those men and women who served in the armed forces of the United States in World War II and so preserved American freedom."[210] The grove remains the largest World War II memorial in America. Unfortunately, the grove marker was overgrown, and "the grove was lost to near-obscurity for many years, as road changes and vegetation growth hid the marker in shadows. The grove marker was recently unveiled and rededicated in 2014 in a new location in the park's day use area, so that this unparalleled monument to our veterans will be remembered and appreciated for generations to come."[211]

In May 1940, the state park system announced that "a new camp area is being prepared in the recently acquired Mill Creek Redwoods in Del Norte

The groves of redwoods north of the Smith River were first known as Hiouchi Redwoods before being renamed Jedediah Smith Redwoods in the 1940s. *HRIA.*

County. The camp will [have] about twelve cabins." The campground opened on the south side of Highway 199 and north of the Smith River, across from the mouth of Mill Creek, with twenty-five campsites. The grove had been donated by Mr. and Mrs. C.M. Goethe in honor of Smith.[212] This facility formed the nucleus of Jedediah Smith Campground. By 1948, the campground had twenty-five campsites. The initial work done on the campground was by the CCC workers, who also built a footbridge across the Smith to access Stout Grove and the Mill Creek Groves. The campground and surrounding redwood groves were renamed in 1951 for American explorer Jedediah Smith, who traveled along the river also bearing his name in 1828. This park grew by 1959 to encompass 8,800 acres of redwood lands. In 1963, reporter Bill Shands in the *San Mateo Times* expressed his opinion that Jedediah Smith was "one [of] if not the best of the California State Parks. Many widely spaced campsites make it a camper's delight. The deep, clear Jed Smith river provides stimulation, [if chilly] swimming and good fishing. And the well-developed, if few, trails make for satisfying hiking."[213] The park now has ninety-three camping sites.

After World War II, there was a rapid increase in the demand for lumber, and as in Humboldt County, there was a rapid increase in logging. Additionally, the number of small mills taking only a few men to operate

Visitors enjoy the tall redwoods along Highway 199 and the Smith River. Many trails allow travelers to explore the redwoods. *CSPA.*

also increased. These mills would cut the trees in an area, saw them into lumber and then move to the next stand of trees. Though smaller operations than the large lumber companies, these "gypo" mills could do significant damage to the redwoods. The operators' mindset of get rich quick and move on meant that they were not interested in reforestation or safe timber harvesting practices. In 1959 in Mendocino, Humboldt and Del Norte Counties, there were "about 300 mills and 400 separate logging operations working in the region."[214] The threat that these logging operations presented to the redwoods was quickly perceived by the Save the Redwoods League, and so it intensified its efforts to preserve the trees before they could be logged. The SRL was successful in preserving a total of 10,429 acres at Jedediah Smith. At Del Norte Redwoods, with the acquisition of the Mill Creek Redwoods in the late 1960s, the park had grown to 31,261 acres by 2018. In 1967, a campground was opened that featured 146 sites along the upper reaches of Mill Creek.

The issue of parks or freeways was another threat to the redwoods in Del Norte County, as it had been for those in Humboldt. Both Del Norte Redwoods on the coast and Jedediah Smith were faced with the loss of trees to widen the road. A plan was submitted by State Engineer J.C. Womack to route the highway away from the park, but the SRL wanted none of the highway to affect the park. Newton Drury, in a letter to the editor of the *Sacramento Bee*, explained the SRL's position: "Every possible effort will have to be devoted to this problem, if we are to save, for a second time, this irreplaceable part of American Natural scenery."[215] Ultimately, the road was widened and rerouted slightly; however, a four-lane highway was not built, as had been proposed.

Working as a ranger at Jedediah Smith State Park was and is a unique experience, given its location in the state and having a wild and scenic river running through it. Ranger I Rick Sermon described his experiences at the start of his career as a ranger at the park. He observed:

> *1981 looked like it was going to be a good year at Jedediah Smith Redwoods State Park. Located in the northwest corner of California this redwood park is the only place on the planet where a wild and scenic river flows through old growth redwood. A truly spectacular place. The staff at the park were young and energetic and were always looking for fun adventures to involve the visiting campers. Fortunately, we had a very supportive Supervising Ranger by the name of Dan Scott. From interpreting the history of ice cream to interpreting the underwater geology of the Smith River, Dan was supportive (with caveats!). Ranger Ken Morse developed a great program entitled "Wild River Water Safety". Looking for a way to get wet on a hot summer day Ranger Phi Rovai and interpreter Sue Rovai developed and aquatic interpretive program which explored the realm of the dynamics of the Smith River from under water. Dan's caveat to this program was that all of us would have to successfully complete a Water Safety Instructor course through the Red Cross. We jumped at the chance and all became certified. Next, we approached the North Coast Redwood Interpretive Association for the purchase of masks and snorkels, and they happily supplied the funding for the program. In order to participate in the program, the kids would have to be of a certain age and show proficiency in the water. I remember one young boy who really wanted to participate but was not that good of a swimmer. There were three of us running the program and it was decided that we would let the youngster participate but that I would stick with him the entire time we were in the river. It was a great summer. Campers and kids learned to be safe and the river; got a basic understanding of river hydraulics and geology and where ice cream came from.*[216]

Near the mouth of Mill Creek lies several large groves of redwoods, including the Veterans Grove, dedicated to the veterans of World War II. *HRIA.*

Sermon ended his career with California State Parks as the redwood coast sector superintendent, working closely with the staff of the redwood national parks and overseeing the redwood state parks from Prairie Creek north. His passion for the parks and seeing that all could enjoy the parks is one of the hallmarks of the rangers who serve in the redwood parks.

Since Sermon first began work at Jedediah Smith, the park has continued to gain in popularity as a campground and a place to discover the redwoods. Filmmakers have also used the redwoods to create extraterrestrial planets, setting the scene for science-fiction thrillers and thrillers. In 1983, the movie *The Final Terror* was filmed at the park, as was George Lucas's *Star Wars: Return of the Jedi.* The tall trees were utilized as the home of the Ewoks, helping to create the planet Endor. More recently, the Smith River and the tall trees along its banks were captured in the science-fiction thriller *Bird Box.* The redwoods continue to captivate no matter how they are seen.

Chapter 6

GRIZZLY CREEK STATE PARK

The most recently created and smallest of the Redwood State Parks in Humboldt and Del Norte Counties is Grizzly Creek State Park, located on the Van Duzen River alongside Highway 36. It is fifteen miles east of Highway 101 and was started with a purchase of 150 acres near the mouth of Grizzly Creek by the State of California. The grove had been owned by the Hammond Lumber Company.

Grizzly Creek was named for the grizzly bears that once roamed the area. Unfortunately for the bears, they were hunted to extinction in the 1860s. The name remained, and the mouth of the creek, where it flows into the Van Duzen River, became a stage stop on the Humboldt-Mendocino route that traveled south at Bridgeville to Blocksburg and Harris. For residents from the eastern portions of Humboldt, it provided a convenient watering stop for the turkey, hog, sheep and cattle drives that were common in the fall of the year as the animals were taken to market.[217]

The parklands were made available to the public in 1943. Work began on building a campground and facilities in 1947, allowing the small campground to open in 1949. In 1953, the *Humboldt Standard* described the park as "only a 'child' as far as age is concerned." However, the paper felt that it was a beautiful facility, as "beneath the dense groves of redwoods thirty campsites are stretched along some 150 acres of land which border the Van Duzen river." Each campsite featured a "rock camp stove complete with grill and stove pipe, a cupboard for the food and a table." Important for the increasing number of the public towing trailers, "plenty of room is provided if space

Grizzly Park opened to visitors in 1943 and features a campground, visitor center and picnic area, as well as several trails and swimming. *CSPA.*

is desired for a trailer or for sleeping." The campground had seen visitation rates of twenty thousand people per year since it opened.

In 1960, Karl Wray, for the *San Clemente Sun Post News*, described his family's stay at Grizzly Creek. He captured why this small campground remains popular with visitors despite being located close to Highway 36:

> One of the nicest was Grizzly Creek Redwoods state park, located beside the crystal clear Van Duzen River east of Eureka. Here you can see the big rounded rocks, clear to the river's bottom, and it's very pleasant for bathing. We hiked along a trail wound along the river bluff, where the big trees grow thickest and the fern form a jungle.

Wray also noted the work of the SRL, observing, "California is fortunate that past leaders fought to save many of the redwood groves that now provide majestic beauty in this area. You only have to see the heavily logged sections to appreciate the cool quiet majesty of the redwoods."[218]

The campground is situated between the Van Duzen River and Highway 36, with several sites along the river. *CSPA.*

Two rangers were stationed at the campground. Glen Jones was the first ranger assigned to the park, working there since the park's opening in 1949. His fellow ranger, Morris Watson, had started work at the small park in 1953.[219] In 1955, the *Humboldt Standard* reviewed the plans State Beaches and Parks had for the redwood parks in Humboldt County. In the article, the paper also explained the duties of the rangers:

> *In the summer, the ranger force is mainly busy serving the traveling public. Their principal duty at all times is to administer and to protect the parks, In the winter they do maintenance work on the trails and campgrounds, cleaning up the grounds, correcting erosion and planning future development.*
>
> *New development work is usually planned by the rangers and then contracted. When it cannot be contracted it is done by hired labor and supervised by the rangers. Roads and parking areas are maintained by the Division of Highways.*[220]

In 1961, Grizzly Creek grew by 84.75 acres. As with the other parks, as land became available, it was often purchased by the state if it was identified as being crucial to the park. Many rangers lived in state housing, including Grizzly Creek, because of the remote locations of the parks.

The rangers' workload increased in December 1964, when the Van Duzen flooded along with the other rivers in Northern California. The rangers were often on their own, as floodwaters closed highways and other resources were assigned to Humboldt Redwoods. In March 1965, the *Sacramento Bee* published a pictorial display of the damage done to the parks in Humboldt County. At Grizzly Creek, a picture shows where "debris has become entangled with the tied down picnic tables....Camping fireplaces, weighing as much as 1,000 pounds were washed 500 feet downstream by the flood water....It was estimated damage in 30 park areas would run as much as $2 million dollars." Another image shows Lyle Keith, "park supervisor... dig[ging] out a picnic table after most of the park was covered with two to four feet of silt during the Christmas Flood. They are being readied for use next summer. One table area will be partially dug out and preserved as a flood exhibit." This exhibit has since been discarded.[221] Another paper, the *Red Bluff–Tehema Times*, illustrated the depth of the silt on the campground roads by showing the park employees standing on the road after the three to four feet of silt had been dug out. Another picture showed bulldozers being used to dig out the silt from the day-use area. The articles were printed in March, as the highways in and out of Humboldt were closed for three months after the flood. Despite the damage, thanks to the hard work of state employees, the campground was open for the 1965 summer season. The park saw 10,116 visitors that summer, only 4,000 shy of the previous year.[222]

Following the flood of 1964, the Save the Redwoods League and the State of California began working to add lands to all of the redwood state parks, and bills were put forth in Congress to purchase and create a Redwood National Park. Grizzly Creek benefited from both, and a section of the bill for the Redwood National Park included purchasing an additional 360 acres to add to Grizzly Creek. Another grove was donated in 1965. In 1966, the State of California started condemnation of 85 acres of Pacific Lumber land to add to the park. In 1967, author Herman Wouk and his wife traveled to Grizzly Creek to dedicate a twenty-acre grove in the memory of their son Abe. At the dedication, Wouk explained:

> *Abe Wouk's life was as brief as the life of these trees is long....My wife and I wanted to express our grief and our love for Abe in some lasting*

and beautiful way....We found a fulfillment of this wish in a virgin grove of California Redwoods. These trees speak straight to the heart in a still and holy language. They murmur that all human life is short...that every hour we live is precious....In this grove, given for ever to the people, these grand trees will always live out their full span, then yield place to new seedlings that will grow on the decay of the fallen giants. That is the cycle of virgin forest-fullness of natural life, and new life from death....This hallowed march of nature is worth preserving. Virgin forest once cut down is lost forever. What better memorial then for a life cut short in one unwary moment, than a grove of virgin forest that will never be cut down.[223]

This grove is located west of the campground and in the spring is filled with trilliums and other wildflowers, and fall colors are found on the hazelnut and willows along the edges of the grove. It is indeed a beautiful grove year round. The following year, another memorial grove was added, this time for Blanche G. Williams and Gertrude D. Graham. This grove was forty-seven acres and was purchased for $35,000.

Camp stoves reminiscent of those built by the CCC workers began to be replaced with metal fire rings in the 1980s. *CSPA.*

In 1969, Grizzly Creek almost doubled in size when the Georgia Pacific Corporation donated 290 acres to the state, the land including 206 acres of old-growth redwood, valued at $6 million. These lands included what is now known as Swimmer's Delight and Pamplin Grove. Robert Pamplin was board chairman for Georgia Pacific. However, the Nature Conservancy, the SRL and the state could not come to an agreement over fees and logistics, so the land was given to Humboldt County. Ultimately, the trees are protected,

Opposite: Herman Wouk and his wife felt that the best memorial for their son would be a redwood grove, attending the grove's dedication in 1967. *CSPA.*

Above: Cheatham Grove is located in an oxbow of the Van Duzen River and was featured in the *Star Wars* movie *Return of the Jedi. Author image.*

and the county added a thirty-site campground to Swimmer's Delight; it has become a very popular day-use area in the summer months. Pamplin Grove is used as a group camp, and many weddings have been held under the redwoods there.

The next gift from Georgia Pacific did end up as a part of Grizzly Creek State Parks. The parcel was west of Grizzly Creek and separated by the Van Duzen from the Swimmer's Delight grove. It was donated by Owen R. Cheatham's family, Cheatham having founded the Georgia Hardwood Company in 1927 and created Georgia Pacific in the 1950s, when it was the fastest-growing businesses in the lumber industry. The grove features a trail and, in the 1980s and 1990s, an environmental campground. Cheatham Grove was also used in the filming of *Star Wars: Return of the Jedi*. Many of the scenes of the speeder bike chase were filmed at Cheatham Grove. The exterior of the grove was featured in the science thriller *Outbreak*. In the movie, helicopters fly along the oxbow made in the Van Duzen around what is Cheatham Grove.

Ranger Rick Johnson added a visitor center to Grizzly Creek State Park during his tenure as ranger in the park during the late 1970s and 1980s. He was very proud of "his" park and worked to enhance the experience for visitors. One summer, he added a terrarium so young visitors could enjoy the live birthing of a garter snake found along the river bar. He enjoyed talking with visitors and sharing about the redwoods. The park has thirty-one campsites, a day-use area and a group camp area, as well as several hiking trails.

In 2020, Grizzly Creek received its largest increase to date. From Pacific Lumber land, some 1,407 acres, lying on the north side of the Van Duzen River between Grizzly Creek and Cheatham Grove, were added to the park. The property was purchased in 1999 and transferred to State Parks recently. For the past two decades, it has been held under the auspices of the Wildlife Conservation Board. According to Supervising Ranger Thomas Valteria, the WCB was "originally created within the California Department of Natural Resources, and later placed with the California Department of Fish and Wildlife. WCB is a separate and independent Board with authority and funding to carry out an acquisition and development program for wildlife conservation. The acquisition triples the size of Grizzly Creek."

Chapter 7

REDWOOD NATIONAL PARK
AND CONCLUSION

From the onset of the Save the Redwoods, a goal for the organization was the creation of a redwood national park. In 1919, the SRL officers listed as their third goal, after raising money to preserve redwood groves and to get the state to protect the redwoods on the highway's right of ways, the creation of a national park protecting the redwoods. This goal finally came to fruition in 1968 with the creation of the Redwood National Park, centered on Prairie Creek, Del Norte Redwoods and Jedediah Smith Redwoods State Parks.

The story of the creation of Redwood National Park begins in 1913, when Charles Willis Ward offered to donate twenty-two thousand acres of redwood timber north of the Klamath River to form a national park. Ward would later become involved with the Save the Redwoods League. Ward was involved in the floriculture business, developing different types of carnations. Prior to his death in 1920, he had four hundred acres of land devoted to the florist industry. His offer was not accepted by the National Park Service, and the status quo continued into the next decade. Most likely, one reason that his offer was not accepted was due to the remote location of the groves and the poor condition of highways in the area, as U.S. Highway 101 had yet to be built. Further, these groves were not yet endangered by logging, so the SRL focused on preserving groves in more threatened areas. Although there were pockets of other owners in the proposed park, it was felt by Ward that they could be purchased and added to the park. Some belonged to the Yurok tribe, but again, the theory was that the land could be purchased and the money given to the Native Americans.

Morris-Sublett logging shown near Eureka—redwood logging continued unabated on private in the 1950s and '60s. *Ted Morris.*

In 1947, Assemblywoman Helen Gahagan Douglas from California put forth two bills to purchase a redwood national park and dedicate it to President Franklin D. Roosevelt. Her legislation failed to make it out of committee, and the plans for a national park again faded away. However, the logging industry experienced a boom in the 1950s as World War II veterans began to purchase homes. More trees were being cut down at a faster rate to meet the increased demand for lumber. Additionally, technology developed during the war also helped to speed up the process. Improved engines made the chainsaws cut faster, significantly reducing the time to harvest a tree. The "Humboldt Cut" was introduced, allowing logs to be felled without damage. Other trees, such as the Douglas fir, became commercially desirable and were logged extensively as well. This increase in logging resulted in a rapid

The damage done by logging, as well as the economic cost of taking so much land out of the lumber companies' hands, made the debate in Congress very heated. *Ted Morris.*

decrease in the amount of virgin timber left in northwestern California. Another issue was the change in logging from selective harvesting, wherein only selected trees were cut, to clear-cutting, in which every tree was cut down, in turn causing a great deal of environmental damage to the land in the form of erosion and destruction of wildlife ecosystems.

With the increased amount of logging, the push to protect more redwoods grew even more impassioned. Talks with President Johnson by members of the SRL led to him requesting a study of the situation from then Secretary of the Interior Stewart L. Udall in 1964. Johnson then sought from Udall recommendations to solve issues raised in the report. Udall recommended:

> *The redwoods are a significant part of our heritage and they need preservation. (2) There is an urgent need to preserve additional acreage of virgin growth in a major redwoods park. (3) It is essential to do this to offset continuing attrition and encroachments and to provide opportunity for future generations to see and enjoy these magnificent forests. (4) Of the original redwoods forest comprising some 1,941,000 acres, about 750,000 acres of old growth redwoods remain. About 300,000 acres are essentially untouched virgin growth of which approximately 50,000 acres*

or 2½ percent of the original redwood forests are protected in California
State Parks. (5) At the present annual rate of redwoods harvesting, about
nine hundred million board feet, all old growth redwoods not protected in
parks will be gone by the year 2000, and probably in 20 to 30 years.[224]

This prediction was very accurate—there are no longer stands of old-growth redwood to be logged. All have been harvested, and no mills in Humboldt or Del Norte can still saw old-growth redwood. They have all switched to being able to mill the second- and third-growth that now come to the mills.

The report was shared with chambers of commerce, state, county and local officials; members of the forest products industry; and other interested groups. Overall, the concept of a redwood national park was well received by the public. However, in Humboldt and Del Norte Counties, whose residents' main source of income was from the timber industry, the populace was not as positive about the need for a park. They feared a severe economic downturn, as the park would be taking land off of tax rolls, as well as causing businesses to close and many to lose their jobs. Prior to the creation of the Redwood National Park, there were close to three hundred mills in Humboldt and Del Norte Counties; now there are fewer than five mills. If the park had not been built, however, the same attrition most likely would have occurred, as there were fewer and fewer places to log.

Following the release of Udall's recommendations, discussions were held to determine the best location and size for a park. In 1966, "President Johnson's special message to Congress on conservation matters included support for the creation of a Redwood National Park." Senator Thomas Kuchel of California introduced a bill, S.2962, shortly after reflecting Udall's and Johnson's recommendations. Advocating for a smaller park, in a different location, Representative Don Clausen of Ferndale introduced House bill H.R. 13011.[225] Hearings were held both in Washington, D.C., and in Humboldt County. However, no action was taken that year.

Adding fuel to the need to preserve the remaining trees in a national park was the ongoing logging of the old-growth trees in the proposed park area. Udall tried to convince "officials of the Rellium Redwood Company…to halt timber harvesting in the area proposed for the park." However, "in a letter of August 18, Harold Miller, president of the company, refused the request to halt cutting." Although Miller was resistant, after a direct appeal from President Johnson, "the five lumber companies involved—Rellium, Georgia-Pacific, Simpson, Arcata, and Pacific—agreed to restrict harvesting operations in the involved areas."[226] All of those mills have closed since the creation of the national park.

During the next year, debate on where and how much land to acquire occupied much of the natural resources committees in Congress. On the West Coast, mill owners were worried about consequences of the new park and logged much of their holdings. In 1968, President Johnson again renewed the plea to create the park. He told Congress in his State of the Union address, "I appeal to you…to help save what is the best and most beautiful in our lives and in our country."[227] This time, he was successful in convincing the senators and congressmen that the need for a Redwood National Park was great, and on "September 9 agreement was announced that fixed the park at 58,000 acres to cost an estimated $92,000,000 for land acquisition." The newly formed national park "was authorized to include three State parks—Jedediah Smith, Del Norte Coast, and Prairie Creek—lands in the Mill Creek, Prairie Creek, Lost Man Creek, Little Lost Man Creek, and Redwood Creek drainages, and approximately 40 miles of scenic Pacific Ocean coastline." Of this land, "approximately 10,900 acres of virgin old growth redwood would be set aside in addition to the groves already preserved in the California State Parks." The parklands selected were chosen as they would help protect the redwoods in the Prairie Creek, Del Norte Redwoods and Jedediah State Parks. Finally, on October 2, 1968, "President Johnson signed the Act creating the Redwood National Park."[228] His wife, Claudia "Lady Bird" Johnson, flew to California in November to dedicate the new park.[229]

The site of the dedication illustrated the need for preserving the redwoods; on one side of the road was a clear cut, where all the trees had been cut down, and it was a desolate sight. Across the road were the tall old-growth redwoods. At the dedication, National Park Service director George Hartzog, in a foreshadowing of the grove being dedicated to her the following year, "introduced the First Lady, referring to her as 'Mrs. Beautification,' and 'Mrs. Conservation,' praising the work she had done to 'stir the soul of America' in preserving natural resources and improving the environment." In her speech, she referred to "Redwood National Park, as the 'crowning moment of a crusade which has lasted two generations.'" One of her claims was "that its establishment would change the local economy from a timber base to tourism." This goal has not been met, as tourism is based on a shorter season than logging, thus employing only seasonal workers. At the dedication, Mrs. Johnson expressed her gratitude to the local redwood timber operators, praising their "cooperative spirit." She observed that support for the project had been worldwide: "Now the dream of nature

Left: Lady Bird Johnson stands with U.S. Congressman Don Clausen in the grove dedicated to her in recognition of her efforts toward redwood conservation. *CPHLSC.*

Below: Former president Lyndon Johnson at the Arcata-Eureka Airport on August 27, 1969. Also pictured are Claudia "Lady Bird" Johnson and President Richard Nixon. *CPHLSC.*

lovers and conservationists is a reality." In seeming awe of the redwoods, Johnson noted, "This is my first visit here, except in my imagination, I've been waiting to come here all my life."[230] She was able to experience the redwoods in 1969 as well.

In 1969, for the first time in Humboldt County history, two presidents came to the area for the dedication of the Redwood National Park. In attendance was President Johnson and his wife and President Nixon and his wife, Pat. Additionally, Assemblyman Don Clauson and then governor Ronald Reagan were present. Thousands gathered at the Eureka-Arcata Airport in McKinleyville to see the arrival of Air Force One and to see the presidents. One attendee at the airport told *Times-Standard* reporter John Read, "It was worth taking a half-day off without pay."[231] The dignitaries then flew by helicopter to Orick, where it was a short drive to the Lady Bird Johnson Grove. President Nixon dedicated the grove to Mrs. Johnson in recognition for her work in conservation and environmental causes. During his speech, Nixon observed:

> *I simply want to say, as I stand here in this magnificent grove of redwoods, that President Johnson and I happen to share a number of things in common. I mentioned them briefly at the airport at Arcata. We both served in the House, in the Senate. We both served as Vice President, and we both served as President of the United States. And there is one other thing I find that we have in common. We both have a great admiration for Theodore Roosevelt who was the President of the United States who first showed an immense interest in the whole field of conservation.[232]*

He continued:

> *But certainly to stand here in this grove of redwoods, to realize what a few moments of solitude in this magnificent place can mean, what it can mean to a man who is President, what it can mean to any man or any woman who needs time to get away from whatever may be the burdens of all of our tasks, and then that renewal that comes from it—to stand here makes us realize the great service that a President of the United States, Theodore Roosevelt, rendered when he put so much emphasis on conservation; that these Congressmen and Senators and Governors have rendered by their support of conservation and that our very honored guest, Mrs. Lyndon B. Johnson, Lady Bird Johnson, has rendered in her work for beautification, and particularly her work with regard to this very grove in which we stand. So today I sign*

From left to right: Pat Nixon, Claudia Johnson and President Richard Nixon, during speeches given at the Arcata-Eureka Airport in 1969. *CPHLSC.*

this proclamation as President of the United States, but I sign it for all of the people of California, for all the people of the United States, in admiration and respect for a great First Lady: Lady Bird Johnson.

Lady Bird Johnson Grove, like Founder's Grove in Southern Humboldt, continues to be a popular site to visit, as it provides easy access to see the tall trees. However, it, like other groves in both Northern Humboldt and Del Norte Counties, was endangered by ongoing logging operations. As a result, "After legal battles and continued public pressure, in 1978, the US government purchased from logging companies over 48,000 acres more land in the Redwood Creek watershed to add to the national park." The addition "included large sections of recently clear-cut hills along the length of Redwood Creek."[233]

The Redwood National Park was designated as a World Heritage Site in 1980. According to the New World Encyclopedia, it received the classification in recognition of its "magnificent forest of coastal redwood trees, the tallest and most impressive trees in the world" and "equally remarkable" marine and land life, and it was further designated an International Biosphere

Lady Bird Johnson Grove is a popular trail to hike and highlights a mixed forest of redwood, fir, hemlock and rhododendrons. *Author image.*

Reserve on June 30, 1983. This designation reflects the unique aspects of the forest, as it includes "two distinctive environments—the coastline of the Pacific, and the mountains of the Coastal Range. The parks' 55 kilometer (34.2 mile) coastline consists of steep, rocky cliffs broken by rolling slopes and broad sandy beaches."[234]

When the national park was created, although it surrounded several state parks, each continued to operate as an individual entity. This changed in 1994 when both entities began being administered as one unit, the two working together. For example, much of the interpretation done in the parks is through the auspices of the National Park Service. The campgrounds, on the other hand, continue to be operated by the State Parks. With the additions and including the land in State Parks, the Redwood National Park now encompasses 131,983 acres. Of those, 71,715 belong to the federal government, while the remaining 60,268 are preserved in the State Parks.

In 2002, the Save the Redwoods League made its largest purchase to date: twenty-five thousand acres comprising the Mill Creek Watershed. The league bought the grove from Stinson Lumber Company, and although much of the land had been clear-cut, it is now protected. Furthermore, in a program called Redwoods Rising, the SRL, State Parks and the National Park Service are working to restore the land and replant the trees that have been logged. The project also calls for the removal of old logging roads and restoration of creeks and streams that were diverted or in some cases buried by logging practices.

One of the trees protected in the Redwood National Park is the Hyperion, current holder of the title "World's Tallest Tree," growing along the banks of Tom McDonald Creek. The tree stands at 380.3 feet, making it taller than the Statue of Liberty by 231 feet, and its width is 15 feet. Its crown is "one of the deepest redwood crowns yet measured." The tree has been measured and studied by professors at Cal Poly Humboldt and was named by naturalists Chris K. Atkins and Michael Taylor. They named the tree "after the Greek Titan Hyperion, the high one." To protect the well-documented tree, the area is off-limits to tourists, due to damage done to its roots as well as the detritus left by visitors.[235] Protecting the forest is a challenging balance between access and safety for both visitors and the trees.

Redwood National Park rangers and California State Park rangers, along with the Save the Redwoods League, continue to work to preserve, protect and restore the redwood forests of Northern California. The 5 percent that has been protected continues to attract visitors, awing all with their size and majesty. Future generations owe a great debt of gratitude to those

The Tall Tree Area of Redwood National Park features a grove of the tallest trees in the park. *Author image.*

The founders of the Save the Redwoods League and other dignitaries stand in front of a redwood in Bolling Grove in 1921. *HRIA.*

who fought to protect the trees throughout the twentieth century. Thanks to the efforts of Madison Grant, J.D. Grant, Newton Drury, John Campbell Merriam, Henry Fairfield Osborn, Laura Perrot Mahan and others, the trees are there to walk under, to enjoy and to appreciate for their uniqueness in the natural world.

NOTES

Introduction

1. Grant, *Saving California's Redwoods*, 1.
2. Grant, "Saving the Redwoods," 91.
3. Curtis et al., *Home of the Redwood*, 19.
4. Ibid., 19.
5. Ibid., 13.
6. Brinzing, oral history, 1961.
7. Thornbury, *California's Redwood Wonderland*, 37.
8. Atwood, "High Sierra and the Redwood Highway," 28.

Chapter 1

9. *Stockton Daily Record*, October 28, 1922, 41.
10. Lowe, "Debunking the Sequoia Honoring Sequoyah Myth," 12.
11. Ibid., 63–64.
12. *Stockton Daily Record*, October 28, 1922, 41.
13. Sillett and Van Pelt, "Redwood Tree Whose Crown May Be," 335–59.
14. Guinness World Records, "Heaviest Forest."
15. Chin, "Redwood Trees Have Two Types of Leaves."
16. Pritzker, *Native Americans*, 2:204.
17. *Memorial and Biographical History of Northern California*, 41.

18. Crabtree, "Redwoods," 283–310.
19. *Pacific Bee*, December 20, 1879, 3.
20. Crabtree, "Redwoods," 289.
21. Engbeck, *Saving the Redwoods*, 217.
22. *Oakland Tribune*, September 15, 1900, 12.
23. Crabtree, "Redwoods," 283–310.
24. *Concord Transcript*, June 8, 1916, 4.
25. *Ferndale Enterprise*, July 6, 1915, 1.
26. *Fortuna Advance*, 1922.
27. *Ferndale Enterprise*, February 27, 1920, 1–4.
28. *San Luis Obispo Morning Tribune*.
29. O'Hara and Service, *Mills of Humboldt County*, 42.
30. Ibid., frontispiece.

Chapter 2

31. *Sacramento Bee*, May 29, 1917, 1.
32. Merriam, "Forest Windows," 733–34.
33. Engbeck, *Saving the Redwoods*, 201.
34. Ibid., 202.
35. Ibid.
36. Ibid., 214.
37. Grant, "Saving the Redwoods," 91.
38. Ibid., 97.
39. Ibid., 109.
40. Ibid. The Tall Tree located at the Tall Trees area in what is now Rockefeller Forest held the distinction of being the tallest redwood until its top was blown down in a windstorm in the 1970s. The tall tree honors now are with Hyperion in Redwood National Forest at 380 feet.
41. *Humboldt Beacon*, September 19, 1919, 1.
42. *Humboldt Beacon*, August 22, 1919, 1.
43. Ibid.
44. *Ferndale Enterprise*, August 10, 1919, 8.
45. *Ferndale Enterprise*, October 3, 1919, 1.
46. *Ferndale Enterprise*, February 27, 1920, 1.
47. *Travel Magazine* (August 1920): 23.
48. Ibid., 24.
49. *Petuluma Argus-Courier*, March 3, 1937.

50. *Ferndale Enterprise*, August 15, 1919, 4.

51. *Air & Space Forces Magazine*, "Namesakes: Raynal Bolling."

52. *Humboldt Standard*, August 1921, 1.

53. Grant, *Saving California's Redwoods*, 10.

54. Ibid., 7.

55. Ibid., 15.

56. Ibid.

57. *Ferndale Enterprise*, June 23, 1922, 1.

58. Ibid.

59. Ibid.

60. Ibid.

61. *Record Searchlight*, September 15, 1923, 1.

62. *Daily Gazette-Martinez*, August 20, 1924, 4.

63. *Santa Rosa (CA) Republican*, April 14, 1924, 4.

64. Ibid.

65. *Sacramento Bee*, November 29, 1924, 19.

66. *Ukiah (CA) Republican Press*, December 10, 1924, 1.

67. *Long Beach Sun*, May 8, 1933, 6.

68. *Sacramento Bee*, January 4, 1923, 21.

69. *Sacramento Bee*, May 23, 1925, 218.

70. *Long Beach Sun*, May 8, 1933, 6.

71. *Petaluma Argus Courier*, October 4, 1932, 3.

72. *Anaheim Bulletin*, May 6, 1933, 3.

73. Myra Nye, *Los Angeles Times*, May 7, 1933.

74. *San Francisco Examiner*, February 12, 1925, 10.

75. *Sacramento Bee*, March 4, 1925, 20.

76. *Napa (CA) Journal*, June 10, 1927, 7.

77. *Los Angeles Times*, September 26, 1926.

78. *Pomono Progress Bulletin*, June 18, 1927, 15.

79. *Sacramento Bee*, June 19, 1929, 8.

80. *Press Democrat* (Santa Rosa), May 31, 1927, 1.

81. *San Francisco Examiner*, April 24, 1927, 76.

82. *San Francisco Examiner*, July 30, 1928, 1.

83. *Daily Courier* (Grant's Pass, Oregon), July 9, 1926.

84. *Sacramento Bee*, June 24, 1931, 17.

85. 2010 California Code, Public Resources Code, Section 5094.33.a.

86. *Sacramento Bee*, September 9, 1931, 16.

87. American Presidency Project, "Franklin D. Roosevelt."

88. *Sacramento Bee*, February 27, 1925, 9.

89. Winje, "Hay Mr. Ranger," 2.
90. *Humboldt Times*, March 16, 1939, 1.
91. *Stephens Grove Flash*, CCC Camp S.P. 32, Company 925.
92. Ibid.
93. *Burlington-Humboldt Camp*, CCC Camp, SP2, Company 925.
94. Ibid.
95. Ibid., 9.
96. Ibid., 10.
97. Ibid.
98. Ibid.
99. Ibid., 11.
100. Turner, *Humboldt County Place Names*, 43.
101. *Oroville Mercury Register*, January 26, 1938, 2.
102. *Fresno Bee*, June 6, 1937, 58.
103. *Redwood City Tribune*, September 9, 1938, 9.
104. French and Drury, oral history, 1963, 1.
105. Ibid., 4.
106. Ibid., 10.
107. Ibid., 26.
108. Ibid., 49.
109. Ibid., 65.
110. *Placer Herald*, January 3, 1942.
111. *Ukiah Republican Press*, December 12, 1945, 3.
112. *Oakland Tribune*, December 11, 1945, 24.
113. *Stockton Evening and Sunday Record*, May 29, 1951, 3.
114. *Sacramento Bee*, November 5, 1953, 25.
115. *Humboldt Standard* (Eureka, CA), October 28, 1955, 1.
116. *Humboldt Standard* (Eureka, CA), June 5, 1959, 17.
117. *Humboldt Standard* (Eureka, CA), August 27, 1960, 1 and 3.
118. *Sacramento Bee*, March 4, 1965, 49.
119. Daniel, "History of the Ave."
120. *Dunsmuir News* (Dunsmuir, CA), July 5, 1972, 1.
121. Baird, oral history, August 10, 2023.
122. Jones, oral history, September 16, 2023.
123. Ibid.
124. *Times-Standard*, June 2, 1991, 1.
125. Pritchard, oral history, 1989.
126. Facebook, "Magical Bucket List Destinations."

Chapter 3

127. *Daily Palo Alto Times*, August 12, 1920.

128. *Fresno Morning Republican*, August 21, 1923.

129. *Petaluma Argus-Courier*, July 31, 1924.

130. Ibid.

131. *San Francisco Chronicle*, May 27, 1923.

132. *Sacramento Bee*, December 29, 1923.

133. Ibid.

134. *Petaluma Argus-Courier*, July 31, 1924.

135. *Sacramento Bee*, January 12, 1926.

136. *San Francisco Examiner*, June 29, 1924.

137. *Napa Valley Register*, June 21, 1927, 6.

138. *Hayward Semi-Weekly Review*, June 29, 1928, 2.

139. *Fort Bragg Advocate and News*, June 29, 1927, 7.

140. Ultrarunning History, "1927 Redwood Indian Marathon."

141. *Petaluma Argus-Courier*, October 9, 1928, 3.

142. *Sacramento Bee*, August 8, 1927, 9.

143. *Oakland Tribune*, May 1, 1927, 40.

144. *The Searchlight* (Redding, CA), December 3, 1929, 2.

145. *Sacramento Bee*, November 1, 1932, 1.

146. Hawk, *Touring the Old Redwood Highway*, 9.

147. *Sacramento Bee*, February 27, 1935, 9.

148. Frank Lyman, *San Francisco Examiner*, August 13, 1933, 57–58.

149. Lou Eichler, *Appeal-Democrat* (Marysville, CA), August 24, 1934, 12.

150. *Yucaipa (CA) News-Mirror*, June 14, 1935, 6.

151. Charles Perrine, *Oakland Tribune*, August 16, 1936, 25.

152. *Los Angeles Times*, October 1, 1937, 2.

153. Ibid.

154. *Santa Rosa Republican*, December 16, 1937, 14.

155. *Mendocino Coast Beacon*, December 25, 1937, 7.

156. Hawk, *Touring the Old Redwood Highway*, 10.

157. Bob Skamser, *Press Democrat* (Santa Rosa), January 1, 1956, 8.

158. *Eureka Humboldt Standard*, July 14, 1959, 11.

159. *Eureka Humboldt Standard*, January 27, 1961, 2.

Chapter 4

160. Irvine, *History of Humboldt County*, 442–47.

161. Morrill, *Humboldt Historian*, 20–24.

162. *Ferndale Enterprise*, August 10, 1923, 1.

163. *Ferndale Enterprise*, July 13, 1923, 1.

164. *Stockton Evening and Sunday Record*, March 12, 1932, 19.

165. *Sacramento Bee*, April 3, 1925, 8.

166. Turner, *Humboldt County Place Names*, 191.

167. *San Francisco Examiner*, May 1, 1932, 61.

168. Ibid., 61–62.

169. *Humboldt Times*, July 2, 1933, 1.

170. *Santa Rosa Republican*, November 11, 1933, 8.

171. *Prairie Creek Prattle*, July 1935, 6.

172. *Humboldt Times*, November 21, 1933, 1.

173. *Ukiah Republican Press*, August 15, 1934, 1.

174. *Prairie Creek Prattle*, CCC Company 1903, October 26, 1934.

175. *Prairie Creek Prattle*, CCC Company 1903, July 1935, 3.

176. *Santa Ana (CA) Register*, August 2, 1941, 2.

177. *The Tribune* (San Luis Obispo), May 31, 1961, 4.

178. *Daily News* (Los Angeles, CA), February 20, 1943, 4.

179. *Long Beach (CA) Sun*, February 20, 1943, 6.

180. *Mendocino (CA) Beacon*, August 24, 1946, 8.

181. *Record Searchlight* (Redding, CA), December 28, 1946.

182. *Sacramento Bee*, July 15, 1948, 2.

183. *Press Democrat*, January 24, 1948, 1.

184. *Sacramento Bee*, January 26, 1948, 11.

185. Matthew Rice, *Humboldt Standard* (Eureka, CA), May 20, 1952, 18.

186. *Humboldt Standard* (Eureka, CA), April 13, 1953.

187. *Petaluma Argus-Courier*, August 10, 1956, 1.

188. *San Francisco Examiner*, May 14, 1873, 1.

189. *Times Standard*, February 13, 1971, 9.

190. *San Francisco Examiner*, February 27, 1881, 2.

191. *San Francisco Chronicle*, May 24, 1892, 3.

192. Rich, oral history, July 19, 2023.

193. *Valley News* (Van Nuys, CA), April 14, 1957.

194. *Times-Standard*, May 11, 1965, 1.

195. *Valley Times* (North Hollywood, CA), June 19 1951, 5.

196. *New York Times*, December 16, 1978, 20.

Chapter 5

197. Coast Redwoods Adventures, "Historic Redwood Logging."
198. *Napa Journal*, January 31, 1928, 6.
199. *San Francisco Examiner*, February 20, 1942, 13.
200. *Peninsula Times Tribune* (Palo Alto, CA), May 13, 1929, 1.
201. Ibid.
202. *Stockton Independent*, May 17, 1926, 3.
203. Knight, "Del Norte Coast State Park," 29.
204. *Sacramento Bee*, May 27, 1931, 26.
205. *Pasadena Post*, December 6, 1937, 3.
206. *Santa Rosa Republican*, May 28, 1935.
207. *San Francisco Examiner*, May 29, 1941, 34.
208. *Sacramento Bee*, February 3, 1942, 6.
209. *Oakland Tribune*, April 22, 1945, 26.
210. Save the Redwoods, "Largest WWII Memorial in U.S."
211. Ibid.
212. *Eureka Humboldt Standard*, June 21, 1958, 7.
213. Bill Shands, "Weekend Camper," *The Times* (San Mateo, CA), August 10, 1963, 29.
214. *Press Democrat*, March 12, 1959, 8.
215. *Sacramento Bee*, December 18, 1963, 80.
216. Sermon, oral history, November 13, 2023.

Chapter 6

217. Turner, *Humboldt County Place Names*, 115.
218. *Sun Post News* (San Clemente, CA), September 14, 1960, 16.
219. *Eureka Humboldt Standard*, July 30, 1953, 14.
220. *Eureka Humboldt Standard*, July 18, 1955, 5.
221. *Sacramento Bee*, March 4, 1965, 49.
222. *Sacramento Bee*, September 2, 1965, 46.
223. *Times-Standard*, July 13, 1967, 3.

Chapter 7

224. Bears, "Redwood National Park History."

225. Ibid.
226. Ibid.
227. *Times Standard* (Eureka, CA), June 30, 1968, 1.
228. Bears, "Redwood National Park History."
229. *Times Standard* (Eureka, CA), August 25, 1968, 1.
230. Bears, "Redwood National Park History."
231. *Times Standard* (Eureka, CA), August 28, 1969, 1.
232. American Presidency Project, "Remarks at the Dedication."
233. National Park Service, "Redwood: Area History."
234. New World Encyclopedia, "Redwood National and State Parks."
235. Famous Redwoods, "Hyperion."

BIBLIOGRAPHY

Books

Curtis, A.A., et al. *The Home of the Redwood: A Souvenir of the Lumber Industry of California, Redwood Lumber Manufactures Association*. San Francisco, CA: D.S. Stanley, 1897.

Engbeck, Joseph H., Jr. *Saving the Redwoods*. San Francisco, CA: Save the Redwoods League, 2018.

Handbook of North American Indians. Vol. 8, *California*. Vol. ed. Robert Heizer. Washington, D.C.: Smithsonian, 1978.

Hawk, Diane. *Touring the Old Redwood Highway, Humboldt County*. Redway, CA: Hawk Mountaintop Publishing, 2004.

Irvine, Leigh. *History of Humboldt County*. Los Angeles, CA: Historic Record Company, 1915.

Jepson, Willis Linn. *A Flora of Western Middle California*. San Francisco, CA: Cunningham, Curtiss & Welch, 1911.

Lynch, Michael. *California State Park Rangers*. Charleston, SC: Arcadia Publishing, 2009.

Memorial and Biographical History of Northern California. Chicago: Lewis Publishing, 1891.

O'Hara, Susan, and Alex Service. *Mills of Humboldt County, 1910–1945*. Charleston, SC: Arcadia Publishing, 2018.

O'Hara, Susan, and Gregory Graves. *Saving California's Coast*. Spokane, WA: Arthur H. Clark Company, 1991.

Pritzker, Barry. *Native Americans: An Encyclopedia of History, Culture, and Peoples*. 2 vols. Ukraine: ABC-CLIO, 1998.

Shepherd, Marvin. *A Scottish Syndicate in the Redwoods*. Walnut Creek, CA: Georgie Press, 2015.

Thornbury, Delmar. *California's Redwood Wonderland: Humboldt County*. San Francisco, CA: Sunset Press, 1926.

Turner, Dennis. *Humboldt County Place Names*. Orangevale, CA: self-published, 2010.

Wallace, Elliott, et al. *History of Humboldt County California, with Illustration*. San Francisco, CA: Wallace W. Elliott & Company, 1881.

Pamphlets

Grant, J.D. *Saving California's Redwoods*. Save the Redwoods League, San Francisco, CA, 1922.

Websites

Air & Space Forces Magazine. "Namesakes: Raynal Bolling." February 25, 2019. https://www.airandspaceforces.com/article/namesakes-raynal-bolling.

The American Presidency Project. "Franklin D. Roosevelt, Message to Congress on Making the Civilian Conservation Corps a Permanent Agency." Online by Gerhard Peters and John T. Woolley. https://www.presidency.ucsb.edu/node/209443.

———. "Remarks at the Dedication of Lady Bird Johnson Grove in Redwood National Park in California." August 27, 1969.

The Ancestor Hunt. "Historical Civilian Conservation Corps (CCC) Newspapers Online." August 4, 2023. https://theancestorhunt.com/blog/historical-civilian-conservation-corps-ccc-newspapers-online.

Coast Redwoods Adventures. "Historic Redwood Logging: Lumber Industry in Del Norte County, 1881–1939." https://www.mdvaden.com/redwood_historic_logging_DN_1881_1939.shtml.

Daniel, Bill. "History of the Ave." Avenue of the Giants. https://theave.org/about-us.

Dymond, Salli F. "The World's Tallest Trees Can 'Drink' Fog." Frontiers for Young Minds, April 1, 2022. https://kids.frontiersin.org/articles/10.3389/frym.2022.676645.

Facebook. "Magical Bucket List Destinations." https://www.facebook.com/profile/100076510402989/search/?q=Humboldt%20Redwoods.

Famous Redwoods. "Hyperion." http://famousredwoods.com/hyperion.

Guinness World Records. "Heaviest Forest." https://www.guinnessworldrecords.com/world-records/634283-heaviest-forest.

Justia—US Law. "2010 California Code: Public Resources Code: Chapter 1.3. California Wilderness Preservation System." https://law.justia.com/codes/california/2010/prc/5093.30-5093.40.html.

National Park Service. "Redwood: Area History," https://www.nps.gov/redw/learn/historyculture/area-history.htm#:~:text=After%20legal%20battles%20and%20continued,the%20length%20of%20Redwood%20Creek.

———. "The Redwoods of Coast and Sierra: Sequoia, Name of the Redwoods." https://www.nps.gov/parkhistory/online_books/shirley/sec3.htm.

New World Encyclopedia. "Redwood National and State Parks." https://www.newworldencyclopedia.org/entry/Redwood_National_and_State_Parks.

Save the Redwoods. "Largest WWII Memorial in U.S. Rediscovered in the Redwoods." September 26, 2014. https://www.savetheredwoods.org/explore/largest-wwii-memorial-in-u-s-rediscovered-in-the-redwoods.

Ultrarunning History. "1927 Redwood Indian Marathon—480 Miles." https://ultrarunninghistory.com/redwood-indian-marathon.

Articles

Atwood, Wallace. "The High Sierra and the Redwood Highway." *Sierra Club Bulletin* 26 (February 1931).

Berrill, John-Pascal, Kevin O'Hara and Nickolas Kichas. "Bark Thickness in Coast Redwood (Sequoia sempervirens (D.Don) Endl.) Varies According to Tree- and Crown Size, Stand Structure, Latitude and Genotype." *Forests* 11 (2020): 637. 10.3390/f11060637.

Chin, Alana. "Redwood Trees Have Two Types of Leaves, Scientists Find—a Trait that Could Help Them Survive in a Changing Climate." The Conversation, April 13, 2022. https://theconversation.com/redwood-trees-have-two-types-of-leaves-scientists-find-a-trait-that-could-help-them-survive-in-a-changing-climate-179812.

Crabtree, Thomas J. "The Redwoods: To Preserve and Protect." *Environmental Law* 5, no. 2 (1975): 283–310. http://www.jstor.org/stable/43265377.

Grant, Madison. "Saving the Redwoods." *New York Zoological Society Bulletin* 22, no. 5 (September 1919): 91.

Knight, Emerson. "The Del Norte Coast State Park." *Sierra Club Bulletin* 16, no. 1 (August 1931): 29.

Lowe, Gary D. "Debunking the Sequoia Honoring Sequoyah Myth." Stanford Digital Library Edition, 2018. https://www.academia.edu/39829981/DEBUNKING_the_SEQUOIA_honoring_SEQUOYAH_MYTH?email_work_card=view-paper.

Merriam, John C. "Forest Windows." *Scribner's Magazine* 83, no. 6 (July 1928): 733–34.

Rohde, Jerry. "Historic Profile of the McKay Tract: Logging, Ranching and Railroads." Prepared for the Humboldt County Public Works Department, March 2014.

Sillett, Stephen, and Robert Van Pelt. "A Redwood Tree Whose Crown May Be the Most Complex on Earth: Trunk Reiteration Promotes Epiphytes and Water Storage in an Old-Growth Redwood Forest Canopy." *Ecological Monographs* 77, no. 3 (August 2007): 335–59.

Van Kirk, Susie. "Prairie Creek Redwoods State Park: A History." September 2015. Prepared for California State Parks.

Newspapers

Anaheim Bulletin. Anaheim, California.

Appeal-Democrat. Marysville, California.

Concord Transcript. Concord, California.

Daily News. Los Angeles, California.

Dunsmuir News. Dunsmuir, California.

Ferndale Enterprise. Ferndale, California.

Fort Bragg Advocate and New. Fort Bragg, California.

Fortuna Advance. Fortuna, California.

Fresno Bee. Fresno, California.

Humboldt Beacon. Fortuna, California.

Humboldt Standard. Eureka, California.

Long Beach Sun. Long Beach, California.

Los Angeles Times. Los Angeles, California.

Mendocino Beacon. Mendocino, California.

Morning Tribune. San Luis Obispo, California.

Napa Valley Register. Napa, California.

Oakland Tribune. Oakland, California.

Oroville Mercury Register. Oroville, California.

Pacific Bee. Sacramento, California, 1899–1900.

Peninsula Times Tribune. Palo Alto, California.

Petaluma Argus Courier. Petaluma, California.

Placer Herald. Rocklin, California.

Record Searchlight. Redding, California.

Redwood City Tribune. Redwood City, California.

San Francisco Examiner. San Francisco, California.

Santa Ana Register. Santa Ana, California.

Santa Rosa Republican. Santa Rosa, California.
The Searchlight. Redding, California.
Stockton Evening and Sunday Record. Stockton, California.
The Times. San Mateo, California.
Times-Standard. Eureka, California.
Ukiah Republican Press, Ukiah. California.
Valley News. Van Nuys, California.
Valley Times. North Hollywood, California.
Yucaipa News-Mirror. Yucaipa, California.

Magazines

Morrill, Don. *Humboldt Historian* (Fall 2016).
Timberman. 1890–1940.

Oral History

Baird, Jim. Conducted by Susan O'Hara, August 10, 2023.
Brinzing, Martin. Conducted by Margaret Pritchard, 1961.
French, Enoch Percival, and Newton Bishop Drury. "Cruising and Protecting the Redwoods of Humboldt." Conducted by Amelia Roberts Fry, Berkeley, 1963.
Jones, Ron, State Park Ranger, retired. Conducted by Susan O'Hara, September 16, 2023.
Pritchard, Harry. Conducted by Susan O'Hara, 1989.
Rich, Sam. Conducted by Susan O'Hara, July 19, 2023.
Sermon, Rick, Redwood Coast Sector Superintendent, retired. Conducted by Susan O'Hara, September 16, 2023.
Winje, Florence Traylor. "Hay Mr. Ranger." Unpublished, available at Humboldt Redwoods.

Miscellaneous

Bears, Edwin. "Redwood National Park History Basic Data, Del Norte and Humboldt Counties California," September 1, 1969, U.S. Department of the Interior, National Park Service. Division of History, Office of Archeology and Historic Preservation.

About the Author

Susan O'Hara was born and raised in Humboldt County, California. She graduated with honors from U.C. Santa Cruz with a double major in history and anthropology and received a Master of Arts degree in history from U.C. Santa Barbara. Over the past thirty-two years, Susan has taught grades K–12 in Humboldt County and has written ten local history books. She is a board member of the Humboldt Redwoods Interpretive Association and the Fortuna Depot Museum Commission and enjoys sharing local history.